CARVING GARGOYLES

GROTESQUES, AND OTHER CREATURES OF MYTH

SHAWN CIPA

Fox
Chapel Publishing

1970 Broad Street • East Petersburg, PA 17520
www.FoxChapelPublishing.com

Carving Gargoyles, Grotesques, and Other Creatures of Myth is an original work, first published in 2009 by Fox Chapel Publishing Company, Inc. No part of this book may be reproduced in any form or by any means, electronic or mechanical, without written permission from the publisher. The patterns contained herein are copyrighted by the author. Copies of these patterns may be made for personal use; however, they may not be duplicated for resale or distribution under any circumstances. Any such copying is a violation of copyright law.

Step-by-step photography provided by Shawn Cipa.

Dedication

To my dear friends Tammy, Jimmy, Tom, Doug, Wendy, and Paula, who have supported and helped me in ways only they could know. Special heartfelt thanks to my dear Trish; her love and devotion know no bounds. To my special Hedy, who reminds me that love is unconditional and frail at the same time. Most of all to God, who has blessed me with this gift of creation.

Acknowledgments

Thanks to Fox Chapel for the opportunity to publish this book. Thanks to all the readers of my books for their much appreciated words of praise. Thanks to Dave Warner for his photography on pages 9 and 13. Finally, thanks to Professor Janetta Rebold Benton and her book, *Holy Terrors: Gargoyles on Medieval Buildings*, which was a great help to me while researching gargoyle history and lore.

ISBN: 978-1-56532-329-4

Library of Congress Cataloging-in-Publication Data

Cipa, Shawn.

Carving gargoyles in wood / by Shawn Cipa.

p. cm.

ISBN 978-1-56523-329-4

1. Wood-carving--Patterns. 2. Gargoyles. 3. Gargoyles in art I. Title.

TT199.7.C554 2009

736'.409892--dc22

2008036834

To learn more about the other great books from Fox Chapel Publishing, or to find a retailer near you, call toll-free, 800-457-9112, or visit us at *www.FoxChapelPublishing.com*.

Note to Authors: We are always looking for talented authors to write new books in our area of woodworking, design, and related crafts. Please send a brief letter describing your idea to Acquisitions Editor, 1970 Broad Street, East Petersburg, PA 17520.

First Printing: November 2008

About the Author

Shawn Cipa began carving wood in 1993. Already possessing a solid background in art, it wasn't long before woodcarving became a driving passion in his life. He began by carving wood spirits, and soon after tried his hand at Old Father Christmas. Although Shawn has carved many different subjects by commission, he admittedly prefers all things whimsical in nature. Walking sticks, canes, Santas, angels, and other mythical characters are just some of Shawn's repertoire.

Shawn comes from an artistic family and has experience in several art forms, such as illustration, painting, and sculpture. Although most art media came easy to Shawn, carving wasn't one of them. It was a daunting task to learn to sculpt by taking *away*, rather than adding on, such as in clay sculpting. However, perseverance has paid off. Scott's other skills include carpentry, photography, and amateur astronomy. Shawn is also an accomplished musician of many years, a passion rivaling his love of the visual arts.

Shawn was recognized as a national winner in Woodcraft Supply Corp.'s 2000 Santa carving contest. He is also the author of *Carving Folk Art Figures, Woodcarving the Nativity, Carving Fantasy & Legend Figures In Wood*, and has been featured in *Wood Spirits & Green Men*, by Lora S. Irish, all of which are available from Fox Chapel Publishing. Shawn has done several how-to articles for *Woodcarving Illustrated* magazine, and continues to provide more of the same. Shawn does commission work from his Website and provides pieces to many collectors internationally. Shawn hopes to continue his carving endeavors with unending support from his family and friends, who have encouraged his efforts.

Please feel free to contact Shawn by visiting his Website at: *www.shawnscarvings.com*.

Beneath the Egyptian goddess, inside the fireplace, two stone gargoyles served as andirons, their mouths gaping to reveal their menacing hollow throats. Gargoyles had always terrified Sophie as a child; that was, until her grandfather cured her of the fear by taking her atop Notre Dame Cathedral in a rainstorm. "Princess, look at these silly creatures," he had told her, pointing to the gargoyle rainspouts with their mouths gushing water. "Do you hear that funny sound in their throats?" Sophie nodded, having to smile at the burping sound of the water gurgling through their throats. "They're *gargling*," her grandfather told her. "*Gargariser!*" And that's where they get the silly name 'gargoyles.'" Sophie had never again been afraid.

—*The Da Vinci Code*, Dan Brown (2003)

Table of Contents

Introduction

The gargoyle often makes his perch
On a cathedral or a church
Where, mid-ecclesiastic style
He smiles an early Gothic smile.
    - Oliver Herford

So, you are casually walking through downtown, or maybe visiting your local house of worship. Perhaps you are on vacation and touring the historical cities of Europe. Look up, and what do you see? Bizarre images staring back at you—some frightening, some humorous, and some just plain weird. Some are so high you can't even see them, but they always see you, watching your every step...

Gargoyles, grotesques, and other stone creatures of fancy have been with us in some form or another since the beginning of recorded history. Even though most people associate them with medieval Europe, these delightful watchers are also found in ancient Egyptian, Sumerian, Babylonian, Greek, and Roman architectural ruins, to name a few. There are also many modern gargoyles all over the world, including cities in the United States. Although the purpose of gargoyles may have changed, they have not lost popularity among those who create them from cold stone. Most were originally created to serve as functional plumbing structures for temples, cathedrals, and other public gathering places, though some homes had them. Although serving ordinary functions, their appearance was anything but ordinary. Artisans and sculptors took great liberty in the gargoyle's aesthetic design—for many reasons it seems, as I will discuss later.

So why, as wood carvers, should we care about the gargoyle? Well, for one, it is a sculptural art form, regardless of the medium. Another reason is the freedom it allowed the sculptor at a time when it was not acceptable for the common artisan to express himself; rather, he was normally bound by strict guidelines. The church commissioned most art at the time, and artists were typically told what to show and how to show it. Artistic license was almost a foreign concept to the medieval artist. The creation of gargoyles, for various reasons, was not bound by the usual restrictions.

Gargoyles give carvers complete freedom of design, without being restricted to conventional anatomical rules. I prefer to carve the fantastic and whimsical: gargoyles provide the perfect outlet. More than that, they can be fun to create! Traditional gargoyles were quite large, for the most part, and were largely exterior in design. The average modern carver would likely work a much smaller scale purely for the enjoyment of carving. You could, of course, carve something more to scale if you so desire, and you could even work it into the architecture of your own home as a shelf, a planter, or a part of a mantle piece over your fireplace.

It is my hope that you, the reader and aspiring carver, will walk away from this book with a new facet of art appreciation you can add and incorporate into your own woodcarving endeavors. Enjoy!
    -Shawn Cipa

History and Lore

To provide some historical knowledge on the subject of gargoyles, I'll examine and explain the different varieties, which has much to do with their design. I will provide some explanation as to why they exist and how they were created, as well as exploring some stories, myths, and legends of these most mysterious stone creatures. I will also provide some information on where the most famous of surviving gargoyles, as well as modern ones, may be found around the world. See page 12 for Part 1: History and Lore.

Chimeras are mythical creatures composed of parts from several species. Well-known chimeras include the gryphon, which has the head and wings of an eagle and the body of a lion, and centaurs, which have the upper body of a human and the body of a horse. Chimeras were popular subjects of grotesques and gargoyles alike. This gargoyle, which shows its waterspout clearly, could represent the original chimera of Greek myth—a mix of a goat and lion, though this specimen also sports wings.

Guardians are statues that are supposed to guard and provide some kind of protection to the building or area they adorn. Sometimes, guardians are also classified as grotesques, depending on the subject matter. The sphinx, though most well known in connection with Egypt, was a guardian often replicated in European and Asian art. These sphinxes are guarding the Whim Garden in Madrid, Spain. The Sphinx is also a chimera with the body of a lion and a human head.

Gargoyles (left close-up) are decorated waterspouts with long necks and troughs that redirect erosive rainwater far from the stone walls of buildings. Cathedrals are popular spots for gargoyles.

Grotesques (middle close-up) are primarily ornamental, though they can be a part of a functional element, such as a corbel (right close-up) or keystone. Decorative grotesques often take the form of an animal, human, or monster sitting or perching on a rooftop.

Step-by-Steps

There are two step-by-steps in this book: the Traditional Water-Spouting Gargoyle and the Classic Grotesque. The carving and finishing processes of these two projects have been broken down and accompanied with detailed photographs so the processes are easy to understand and complete. Key stages of carving are emphasized to ensure that you are on track. Tools and materials lists lay out just what you will need to carve and finish both projects. I've also shared two special finishing styles I created just for these projects. See page 30 for Part 2: Step-by-Steps.

The Traditional Water-Spouting Gargoyle, page 30.

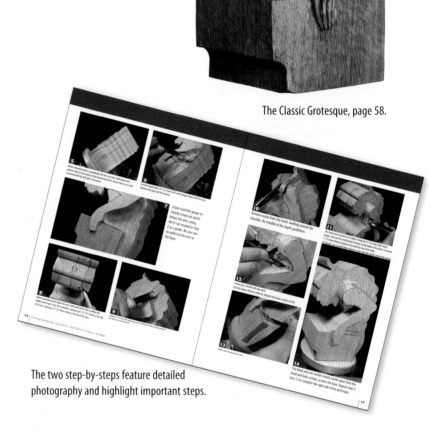

The Classic Grotesque, page 58.

The two step-by-steps feature detailed photography and highlight important steps.

Appendix: Tools and Wood

The tools and wood appendix discusses the use of tools and techniques from a woodcarver's point of view, as opposed to the viewpoints of the stone sculptor of the past. I will offer several finishing options, which, as wood carvers, is something of significance to us. I also discuss the variety of woods I have used in this book, just to mix it up a bit—I invite you to do the same. See page 152 for the appendix.

The appendix discusses tools and techniques.

Projects

The heart of this book is 10 additional gargoyle, grotesque, and guardian carving projects. Besides the projects that are purely ornamental, I've incorporated the subjects into a wide range of architectural elements, such as the Screaming Keystone Grotesque, the Green Man Door Knocker, and the Gargoyle Cane. Each project includes full-page patterns, reference photos of the finished piece taken from multiple angles, a brief discussion of lore relating to the piece, and an explanation of my approach while creating the piece. This "artist approach" discusses important or difficult aspects of carving each piece and includes several photos to illustrate those steps. The designs I've created are my attempt to reflect the different types of gargoyles and grotesques in their most traditional forms, and to provide a few that are not. After all, we are not as bound to convention as our predecessors were. See page 86 for Part 3: Projects.

The Screaming Keystone Grotesque, page 86.

The Guardian Grotesque, page 92.

The Green Man Door Knocker, page 100.

The Corbel with Grotesque, page 108.

The Crouching Imp, page 114.

The Intaglio Lion Medallion, page 122.

The Demon Gargoyle, page 128.

The Gargoyle Cane, page 134.

The Chimera, page 140.

The Woodcarver, page 146.

Part 1
History & Lore

Gargoyles, for most people, immediately invoke the image of a crouched, demonic-looking figure hanging over the ledge of a building, his leering face a visage of terror. It appears as if, at any moment, he will swoop down from his lofty perch, beating his great bat-like wings to attack an unsuspecting victim below. Although some gargoyles are fashioned in this manner, this particular image is a more modern one, romanticized from the influence of fantasy art, literature, movies, and even cartoons.

The term "gargoyle," technically referring to a waterspout, is often used to describe several different types of fantastic sculptures of human or animal form. Grotesques, non-waterspout sculptures that can be carved as part of a functional element or as a stand-alone decoration, are often lumped into the "gargoyle" category. Guardians are a type of sculpture placed at the entrance of buildings to protect them—guardians can be grotesques, but are not always. Chimeras, or creatures with parts from several species, are often cast as gargoyles, grotesques, or guardians.

Gargoyles perch high on buildings and capture the imaginations of those who see them. This screeching gryphon dwells on the Sacré-Cœur Basilica in Paris, France.

This true gargoyle is located at the Pena National Palace, in Sintra, Portugal. Note the water trough carved along the back of the gargoyle. This channel leads to the mouth, which directs the water away from the walls and prevents erosion.

The more gargoyles funneling water from a rooftop, the less chance there is for spillover and accidental erosion. This line of gargoyles perches on the south façade of the Cathedral of Notre-Dame in Paris.

What is a gargoyle?

True gargoyles are actually waterspouts or gutters designed to divert erosive rooftop water away from the walls and foundations of buildings. The English word gargoyle comes to us from the French word *gargouille*, which in turn, comes from the Latin *gargula*, meaning gullet or throat. The first gargoyles were simple, unadorned troughs placed on rooflines, corners, and at the end of flying buttresses (a means of support for the high walls of cathedrals). Anywhere water would gather would be an ideal place for a gargoyle. Although the concept of carving these functional waterspouts into something decorative was not foreign to ancient cultures such as the Egyptians and the Greeks, this practice first became popular in Europe during the beginning of the twelfth century and flourished in the Gothic era (mid-twelfth through fifteenth centuries).

The true gothic gargoyle was a horizontally protruding structure depicted as a fantastic creature. The neck was often quite long, ending with a head sporting a gaping mouth. A trough was cut along the length of the gargoyle; water flows through this channel and out of the mouth. The beasts, clinging to the side of the building with their claws, appeared to be spitting or vomiting water, outstretched as far as they could possibly reach. Architects soon realized that the more they divided the water flow, the more they reduced the potential damage to each building. As a result, armies of gargoyles were spread along entire rooftops. The Cathedral of Notre-Dame in Paris and the Old Cathedral of Utrecht in the Netherlands are good examples.

Several architectural points were common locations for gargoyles. One, the flying buttress, provided an ideal location for a waterspout. Flying buttresses were used to redirect the support of a wall to an outside pillar. This permitted large openings in the walls, such as stained glass windows, that otherwise would have greatly weakened the structure. These gargoyles and accompanying flying buttresses are a part of the Church Notre-Dame of Strasbourg in France.

Photo courtesy of Chonoi.

The Vampire of Notre-Dame, also known as Le Stryge, sports an entire body from the waist up, which seems to be common among the grotesques found at Notre Dame cathedral in Paris.

This corbel, supporting the roof of a building in Auxerre, France, features a full-bodied grotesque carved from wood.

Photo courtesy of Mattana.

What is a grotesque?

The term "gargoyle" has come to be an inaccurate catchall word for all fanciful animal sculpture found upon the rooftops of medieval buildings. Many of these do not serve as waterspouts, but perform some other function or are decorative in nature. These are correctly referred to as grotesques. Probably one of the most recognizable grotesques is the Vampire of Notre-Dame, found at the Cathedral of Notre-Dame in Paris, France.

Grotesques exist in many forms and in many architectural locations. Some are full-bodied, some are only heads or faces. Faces are commonly found on the center keystone of an arched entranceway. Another common location for grotesques are corbels—a type of fancy bracket that protrudes from a wall and is used to support a variety of architectural elements, such as roofs, beams, mantels, and even water-spouting gargoyles themselves. Capitals, or the area at the top of a column where the column contacts the surface it is supporting, are another part that carvers decorated with grotesques.

Artisans of the past seemed willing to find a place just about anywhere for grotesques, from corbels to molding to door knockers. Regardless of the form, grotesques are unlimited in their variety of presentation. Some are frightening, with toothy grimaces and furrowed brows; some are humorous, picking their noses or pulling at their facial features; and some are straightforward, with attractive visages (mostly religious in nature), although this was far less common.

Photo courtesy of Ken Thomas.

The two lion sculptures in front of the New York Public Library, carved in 1911, are modern examples of lion guardians.

What is a guardian?

Another form associated with gargoyles and grotesques is the guardian. Guardian statues are not strictly grotesques, but I have chosen to include them because of their often fantastical nature, and they are also often found in the same places. Guardians were most often placed at entranceways to protect palaces, residences, and tombs of royalty. The guardian concept dates far back to the beginning of recorded civilization. By far, the most popular subject for the classic guardian is the majestic lion, winged or otherwise. He is usually portrayed in the upright sitting position. Ancient China had its own version—the Imperial Guardian Lions of the Forbidden City (see page 28). Other popular subjects for the guardian were dragons and soldiers riding horses.

Photo courtesy of Johannes Otto Först.

The Green Man is a commonly portrayed grotesque. The Green Man corbel at the Bamberg Cathedral in Bavaria, Germany, might be the most well-known example of a Green Man.

Popular subjects

Gargoyle, grotesque, and guardian carvers have certainly not been unimaginative with their creations. The subjects of these Gothic stone works are sometimes surprising, but always interesting. These sculptures, spread throughout the world, feature an incredible range of people, animals, and mythic creatures.

Green Man

The Green Man is most definitely a significant element of the grotesque category. Most woodcarvers are quite familiar with the Green Man, and no doubt many of you have tried your hand at carving one. This leafy guy was actually quite popular architecturally, and is found in countless places around the world. Although the Green Man has his roots in pagan belief systems, he is also integrated into many designs of religious structures. The Green Man was a Druidic god-form of tree worship, a representative of the unseen power of nature. Probably the most famous of these is the Green Man corbel of Bamberg, found in the Bamberg Cathedral in Bavaria, Germany. The Green Man is everywhere in southern England.

Animals

Animals, in varying degrees of true anatomical form, were used often as grotesques and gargoyles alike. Goats, monkeys, pigs, lions, and birds were popular subjects—even elephants and the unlikely rhinoceros were used. Dogs seem to be the most popular animal carved in medieval times. Animal carvings were usually meant to symbolize negative and positive aspects of man's nature, as interpreted by the church. For example, cats and foxes were associated with vanity and sneaky behavior, so they were symbols of the devil. Lions, bulls, and eagles were symbols of majesty and honor, and have been associated with Christian saints. The dog symbolized loyalty, which nicely represented the humble and vigilant servant of Christ and the Church.

Chimeras

Composite creatures found guarding entranceways, perching on rooftops, or carved on pillars are called chimeras—figures composed of parts from different species. Medieval artists were fond of creating fantastically imaginative sculptures composed of the face of one creature, the feet of another, the rear end of a third, and on and on in endless variation. The Sphinx is probably the most famous chimera guardian in ancient Egypt. An older version used by the Mesopotamians sported a bearded man's head on a winged lion's body. Greeks and Romans depicted a female version. Another popular chimera subject was the gryphon—a beast with the body of a lion and the head and wings of an eagle.

Photo courtesy of Simon Garbutt.

Animals were popular subjects for grotesques and gargoyles. These two corbels from the Church of Saint Mary and Saint David in Kilpeck, Herefordshire, England, are decorated with a ram and a lion.

Photo courtesy of Nino Barbieri.

The popular gryphon chimera guards many buildings, including Saint Mark's Basilica in Venice, Italy.

Why do gargoyles and grotesques look like they do?

Why was so much ornamentation bestowed on something as common as plumbing? Why were multitudes of bizarre, silly, ugly, and frightening images crawling all over the eaves of holy sanctuaries? Why did church officials spend so much effort and money to have them created? The original purpose and meaning of gargoyles is unknown, and has largely been lost to modern man. It is unlikely there is one meaning for all the stone creations, but rather an amalgamation of many, some more plausible than others. Nevertheless, I will attempt to explain the most popular theories.

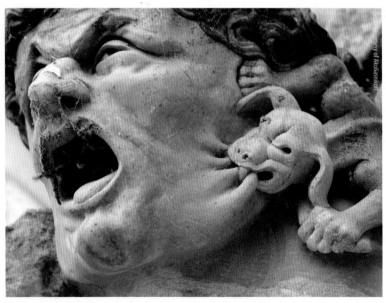

There are many theories as to the appearance of gargoyles. One thought is that they symbolize condemned souls. This gargoyle on Salisbury Cathedral, Salisbury, England, is a good example of a tormented soul.

Encouraging faith

The foremost thought in most people's minds is that gargoyles are demons. This may be a plausible concept given their appearance, but then why would the heads of the Church allow such monstrosities to adorn a temple of God? There are several possible reasons, based on religious education of the public.

Serving as symbols of evil forces, such as sin and temptation, gargoyles lurked outside the sanctuary, creating a gauntlet the visitor had to pass while entering inside. Once inside, the visitor was safe, and he or she had symbolically resisted temptation. The devil was said to be always watching the potential sinner, just as gargoyles looked down on those below.

Another theory is that some gargoyles represent condemned souls not allowed inside the church. They had been spared from hell, but were turned to stone as punishment for their sins—though this does not explain why some grotesques were found inside churches. Either way, they served as reminders to the parishioners of what could happen to them. It was a popular belief of the Middle Ages that if the love of God did not stop people from wanting to sin, then the fear of hell surely would. Based on this concept, it became the artist's responsibility to help influence public behavior by carving the most frightening images possible.

The Green Man was an important part of many pre-Christian cultures. As a means to draw pagans into churches, Green Men and other pagan gods were incorporated into cathedral architecture. This Green Man is carved above an entrance into Southwell Minster in England.

Encouraging conversion

It is also widely believed that gargoyles and grotesques found on religious structures may have roots from pre-Christian pagan belief systems. During the 1200s, the Roman Catholic Church was very keenly interested in recruiting non-believers into the faith. Virtually no one in the common ranks (as well as a large part of the clergy) could read, so any available printed literature was of little use. Imagery was the main teaching tool in those days. For this reason, the gospel was preached largely through the erection of elaborate stained glass scenery and sculpture. Pre-Christian cultures had many gods and goddesses, most of which were drawn from nature itself. Half-animal and half-human forms, which are embodied in many existing gargoyle sculptures, could

possibly reflect these deities of the distant past. The archetypal Horned God of ancient pagan belief and the Green Man are two examples of pagan gods represented in gargoyle or grotesque form.

In order to convert the populace to the Christian faith, draw them in, and make them feel more comfortable, gargoyles may have been created as representatives of these pagan gods. The blending of pagan beliefs into Christian ones was a common method of conversion during the Middle Ages. For example, the birth of Christ was positioned around the same time that the winter solstice was celebrated in many existing pagan traditions. Many compromises of this manner were made in order to fill the pews come Sunday.

One possible explanation for the fantastic nature of some gargoyles is that the sculptors were influenced by the discovery of dinosaur fossils. This dragon-like sculpture adorns a building at the University of Chicago in the United States.

Protection

As a twist, another theory is that gargoyles and grotesques were guardians of the church. They served as scarecrows to frighten off other evil forces, deterring demons by proclaiming, "Don't bother, we're already here doing evil stuff." This would explain why the artist attempted to make his creation as ugly as possible. It was thought some of the gargoyles would come alive after dark and fly about the premises to keep watch. No one could see after nightfall, so no one could prove it didn't happen!

Archeological influence

Yet another theory is that gargoyle and grotesque sculptors were inspired by the discovery of prehistoric skeletal remains—yes, dinosaurs. Dinosaur bones were probably found all across Western Europe during the Middle Ages, and scholars of the time struggled to explain their existence. The discoveries were no doubt a thorn in the side of the church officials, and many crackpot theories were fabricated. No surviving documentation of these practices exists; nevertheless, it is possible the dinosaur fossils provided fodder for the imagination of artists.

Entertainment

Another plausible explanation for the creation of so many of these fantastic designs is for purposes of entertainment. In the days of illiteracy, gargoyles most likely provided much entertainment to the public—thrills of horror and laughs alike.

Fascination with the macabre is a social phenomenon that remains popular today. Consider today's huge attraction to the horror genre—movies, books, comics, cartoons, even the celebration of Halloween. Modern culture has built themes around nasty creatures such as vampires, werewolves, and a plethora of other monsters beyond description. Slasher films, containing murderous characters such as the chainsaw-wielding Leatherface, are actually considered great fun to watch, and are known internationally. During the Middle Ages, the allure of horror was no different. In fact, people of the time probably felt even more of a connection to these images as an expression of their own subconscious fears, as opposed to the desensitization of today. The medieval artists who created countless gargoyles and grotesques were the Stephen Kings of their own time.

However, not all gargoyles provided a good scare; some provided a good laugh instead. Satire played an important role in daily medieval society. Most humorous gargoyles were of a human nature, and were more often bizarre than attractive. Some are shown to engage in activities beyond the bounds of socially acceptable decency, which may seem surprising, but it is a misconception that the Middle Ages were a time when fun was not allowed. One annual festival, the Feast of Fools, started on the first of January and lasted for a few

This amusing gargoyle on the Basilica Saint-Urbain in Troyes, France, appears to be vomiting or drooling when spouting rain-water.

days. The social hierarchy was reversed during this time, and the commoners would "elect" their own heads of church. Singing, dancing, indulgence, and obscenity were the order of business during the celebration. Ironically, this was not an affront to the church—the celebration actually took place within the church walls. It was a way for the church to retain its authority by keeping an eye on the debauchery.

Satirical gargoyles were a reflection of this controlled debauchery. There are many human gargoyles known as face pullers, recognizable by the subject's hands pulling at their own open mouths, thereby stretching the opening even wider. It was a funny sight to see rainwater issuing from the face-puller's mouth, as if he were drooling or vomiting. Alarmed passersby below doused by the issuing water would quickly realize the prank that was being pulled. All in observance would then share a chuckle!

How were gargoyles and grotesques created?

The tools used to create stone sculptures in the Middle Ages were probably not much different than those used by today's stonemasons. Though many today use pneumatic (compressed air) tools for the roughing-out process, the details are usually still done with hand tools. Such tools as used by the medieval stonemason would include a large wooden mallet, a variety of iron chisels, files, and calipers to gauge measurements.

Artisans developed their ideas by constructing small-scale models out of clay or plaster. Once the design was satisfying, the artist would begin roughing out the stone block. It must be remembered that most gargoyle carvings were quite large, but were also a great distance from the viewer below.

For this reason, features of the gargoyle were exaggerated and details were sometimes simplified and deeply undercut so that they could be distinguished. Most medieval gargoyles were carved of limestone and marble, but other materials, such as wood and terra-cotta, were used on occasion. No wooden gargoyles survive today, though there are a few wooden grotesques from medieval times, and very few terra-cotta gargoyles have stood against the centuries of corrosive weather. A few rare leaden gargoyles still exist, but they are more common to the sixteenth century and forward.

Most gargoyles were carved on the ground—either in the courtyard (weather permitting), or in the studio. It would have been quite dangerous to try to carve one already in place. Some are found in the most awkward and elevated of places, and there would have been constant debris showering passersby as the carver worked. On the rare occasion a mason carved the details in place, it would be because the hoisting process might damage a design element.

The actual artistic portion of the gargoyle that was visible was only the tip of the iceberg, so to speak. It was carved from a much larger single block, half of which was put in place as part of the wall, cornice, or ledge that it was to be displayed on. This was necessary for stability: the unseen portion served as a counterbalance so the figure could project out into open air without danger of crashing to the ground below. Imagine how difficult it must be for today's masons who dedicate themselves to restoring or replacing an existing work that is part of the building's structure.

The years' worth of erosive rainwater that have poured through a gargoyle often destroy at least part of the sculpture. This stone gargoyle on Troyes Cathedral, in Troyes, France, shows the effects of weather; imagine how quickly a wooden or terra-cotta gargoyle would erode.

Some gargoyles were fitted with pipes to minimize erosion, like this one on Prague Castle.

Once the gargoyle was completed, it was put into place. Most weighed a few hundred pounds at the very least; many were probably half a ton or better. A hoisting device, known as a windlass system, was used to lift the piece vertically, as scaffolding was unknown to workers of the Middle Ages. A windlass system consisted of a barrel or cylinder that could be rotated by a crank. Combined with ropes and pulleys, a windlass system could lift very heavy objects. (Incidentally, windlass systems had many uses during medieval times, notably as weaponry and torture devices.) Once in place, the mason might put final touches on a carving after he was able to view it from below.

Most gargoyles and grotesques were painted with bright and gaudy colors, which must have had a quite different effect from what we are used to seeing. Some were gilt. As you would imagine, the paint did not last very long because of constant exposure to the elements.

The destruction and restoration of gargoyles is a constant battle. Some functional gargoyles were fashioned with lead or iron pipes protruding from their mouths in an attempt to minimize corrosion from passing rainwater. Many of those still existing today have been proactively outfitted with modern drainage systems, which somewhat diminishes the gargoyle's aesthetic appearance. Acid rain, pollution, and airborne chemicals all contribute to the slow destruction of these invaluable pieces of history. Bird droppings and dirt sometimes clog the drainage channels of the gargoyles; combined with constant watering, plants often grow. The root systems of the plant life is yet another cause of damage to the stone. It is unfortunate that many gargoyles are steadily being destroyed by time, despite the attempt of many workers to restore them. Many gargoyles have been replaced; even now, some of the replacements are growing old. It is sometimes almost impossible to tell which ones are not original, which is a testimony to the great skill of those masons who dedicated themselves (and still do) to the task of restoration.

Where can gargoyles and grotesques be found?

There are hundreds of wonderful places around the world to see fine examples of gargoyles and grotesques, places you might not expect. From Western Europe to the Middle East, Asia, and the United States, these fantastical creatures abound in an endless variety of shapes and designs. I certainly cannot touch on them all, but I would like to mention a few of the more well-known places to visit—whether it be by actual globetrotting, or merely by Internet-surfing from the comfort of your favorite armchair.

Western Europe

The most impressive medieval gargoyles are found at the great Roman Catholic cathedrals of Western Europe, such as those of France. The Cathedral of Notre-Dame in Paris, probably the most famous cathedral in the world, is a fine example of high Gothic design. This is the home of the most famous of grotesques—the Vampire. Notre-Dame sports an array of the finest examples of gargoyles and grotesques, many of which were destroyed or removed during the French Revolution. A man named Eugène Viollet-le-Duc restored most; his work began in 1845. The cathedral was again restored between 1991 and 2001, and some work still continues. Many original water-spouting gargoyles remain along the flying buttresses; however, the wear and tear shows profoundly on some.

The next best example of high-Gothic architecture, complete with flying buttresses, is the Chartres Cathedral, also in France. Approximately 4,000 sculpted figures adorn the cathedral, most of which are religious in nature. Literally hundreds of grotesque designs clutter the overhead archways of the entrances, or portals. The best-known sculpture at Chartres is engraved above the central portal in a type of deep-relief style. It is quite a complex design, and depicts Christ in majesty, surrounded by the four apocalyptic beasts of Revelations. The decorum at Chartres is most impressive to behold, and a must-see if you happen to visit France.

One more location in France I must mention is the Vézelay Abbey, otherwise known as the Basilica of St. Magdalene. Once thought to hold relics of Mary Magdalene herself, this outstanding example (possibly the finest) of Romanesque artistry is found in the Burgundy region. Built around the early 1100s, Vézelay contains loads of grotesque sculpture within its walls. Most notably, there are many columns inside that are highly sculpted with complicated scenes depicting stories, myths, and religious events. The carvings themselves feature many fantastic-looking creatures, beasties, and demons of true grotesque style.

The United Kingdom has seemingly countless locations with gargoyles and grotesques; some buildings contain just a few fine examples, while others have many. Again, it is impossible to mention more than a fraction of these locations.

Oxford University in Oxford, England, founded during the 1300s, has many fine Gothic gargoyles. The University at Oxford is not one unified campus; rather, it is a collection of many colleges and buildings, both old and newer. This scholastic wonderland is a treat to explore on foot, and there is much architecture to examine. If you decide to visit, take binoculars—most of the gargoyles and grotesques are located very high from the ground. The university has produced some famous fantasy authors, among them Lewis Carroll (author of *Alice's Adventures in Wonderland* and its sequel *Through the Looking-Glass*), C. S. Lewis (*Chronicles of Narnia*), and J. R. R. Tolkien (*Lord of the Rings*). One can't help but wonder if the picturesque surroundings and Gothic sculptures helped to spur these most creative minds.

York Minster in York, England, is an imposing Gothic cathedral of Norman design that dates back to the mid-twelfth century. The cathedral is known for its impressive stained glass windows, some dating back to the structure's origin. York Minster is a wonderful place to view waterspout gargoyles and interior grotesques, some humorous, and some quite spooky. The place is riddled with Green Men, as well as human head grotesques. In my opinion, the most impressive carving is found in the crypt below the main altar. On display is a relief-carved limestone slab known as the Doomstone. It is a depiction of the Last Judgment, and shows a cauldron into which damned souls are being pushed and tortured. Demons and flames abound, as well as many symbolic figures. The subject is quite grisly; however, the piece is extremely detailed and is a wonderful example of early medieval artistry. The prospect of the tortures of hell was an intimate reality to the people of this age, and this carving shows it.

In Venice, Italy, be prepared for utter amazement when visiting the Basilica of San Marco (Saint Mark). This church is the most famous in Venice, and is a mixture of Gothic, Byzantine, and Romanesque architectural styles. From its richly adorned mosaic interiors to the highly carved spires and domes, the Basilica is home to countless gargoyles and grotesque sculptures. It seems every inch of exterior surface is carved in some form. Truly breathtaking!

The University Church of St. Mary the Virgin is part of Oxford University. The tower, which dates from 1315, is covered with gargoyles.

The Basilica of San Marco, in Venice, Italy, is home to countless gargoyles and grotesques. Numerous human grotesques perch on the top of the front arches, while human gargoyles carry water jugs with pipes to release rainwater.

Allen Timothy Chang.

Fierce lions make good guardian figures. The Imperial Guardian Lions watch over the Forbidden City in Beijing, China.

Photo courtesy of Gisin.

A pair of mythical kinshachi adorn the donjon, or castle keep, of Nagoya Castle in Nagoya, Japan. These grotesques are so famous that the castle has been nicknamed *Kinshachi-jo,* meaning "Kinshachi Castle."

Asia

When one thinks of gargoyles, the Far Eastern influence rarely comes to mind. Nevertheless, some of the most impressive gargoyle and grotesque artistry can be found throughout countries of Asian heritage. Highly detailed, painted carvings were more often carved of wood than of stone, and have been carefully preserved or restored over the long ages. Many were also cast in bronze or other metals.

The most known site may well be the Forbidden City in Beijing, China. The Forbidden City was built in the 1400s during the Ming Dynasty, and served as the seat of Imperial authority, as well as the personal dwelling of the emperor. Commoners were not allowed to enter the city, thus its title; today all of the city is open to tourists, and is considered a national museum. Within the city, at the Gate of Supreme Harmony, there are two incredibly huge bronze imperial lion guardians flanking the stairway. On the west side is the empress lion, with a cub under her paw. To the east is the emperor lion, with the world under his.

The eaves of castles all over Japan are decorated with *kinshachi*—chimera grotesques shaped like fish with tiger heads. These mythical creatures were believed to protect the buildings they adorned from fire. Nagoya Castle, in Nagoya, Japan, has two very large kinshachi on its roof. The male and female pair is nicknamed the Golden Dolphins. The grotesques are about $8^{3}/_{5}$ feet (2.6 meters) tall, weigh around 2,800 pounds (1,270 kilograms) each, and have 238 combined scales made from 18-carat gold.

United States

The United States contains some fine examples of gargoyles, even though they are more modern than in most other parts of the world. The National Cathedral in Washington, D.C., first erected in 1907, took 83 years to build to completion. It is the second largest cathedral in the United States, and has several decidedly modern gargoyles and grotesques among the many more traditional ones. There are also many satirical and humorous sculptures. The carvings there are quite detailed and artistic, and the subject matter is quite varied. There are the expected dragons, chimeras, and winged demons. There are many animals beyond the typical, such as an alligator, poodle, seal, sea turtle, squirrel, hamster, and caterpillar. There is even a housefly clutching a can of insect repellent. Many humanistic examples of a social nature adorn the building, including a lawyer, crooked politician, dentist, caveman, and a sleeping hippie. Some portray socio-political states such as hatred, famine, and adoration. There are carvings of obviously modern reflections, such as a "big brother" camera and a robotic computer. There is even a carved portrait of Star Wars arch-villain Darth Vader.

Guardians and grotesques abound on older buildings throughout Manhattan, and cathedrals there are quite likely to harbor gargoyles.

If you look around your local metropolis, you're sure to find a gargoyle or grotesque hiding somewhere among the rooftops. In this photograph from 1920, three workers admire a grotesque perched on Old City Hall in Toronto, Canada.

At a location near you

Aside from the famous places I have mentioned throughout the globe, you may find a gargoyle or grotesque dwelling right in your hometown or neighboring city. Keep your eyes open and look around, especially in metropolitan areas. You will undoubtedly find a small face lurking somewhere, staring out at all the passersby, who in their daily haste have forgotten to appreciate the influence of history on the present.

The author gratefully acknowledges his debt to Professor Janetta Rebold Benton's book, *Holy Terrors: Gargoyles on Medieval Buildings*, Abbeville Press, NY, 1997 (French edition, *Saintes Terreurs: les gargouilles dans l'architecture médiévale*, Éditions Abbeville, Paris, 1997, second edition 2000). Professor Benton has written a truly fascinating and good source on gargoyle history. Any readers looking for further historical information should check her book first.

Additional recommended sources on gargoyle history and lore include Time Life Records' 2005 DVD, *Gargoyles: Guardians of the Gate*; sculptor and stone carver Walter S. Arnold's Web site (www.StoneCarver.com); and sculptor and stone carver Joe Chiffriller's Web site (www.NewYorkCarver.com).

The Traditional Water-Spouting Gargoyle Step-by-Step

Our first project is closely modeled after the traditional gargoyles found at French cathedrals, such as Notre Dame. The basswood block I use measures 14" x 6" x 4" (35.6cm x 15.2cm x 10.2cm). It is large, but I think carving the piece any smaller would diminish its impact. Actually, after you have mastered this project, it would be awesome to convert it to a much larger size—perhaps two or three feet long (61cm or 91cm). Mounted on an outer wall somewhere, it would definitely get people's attention!

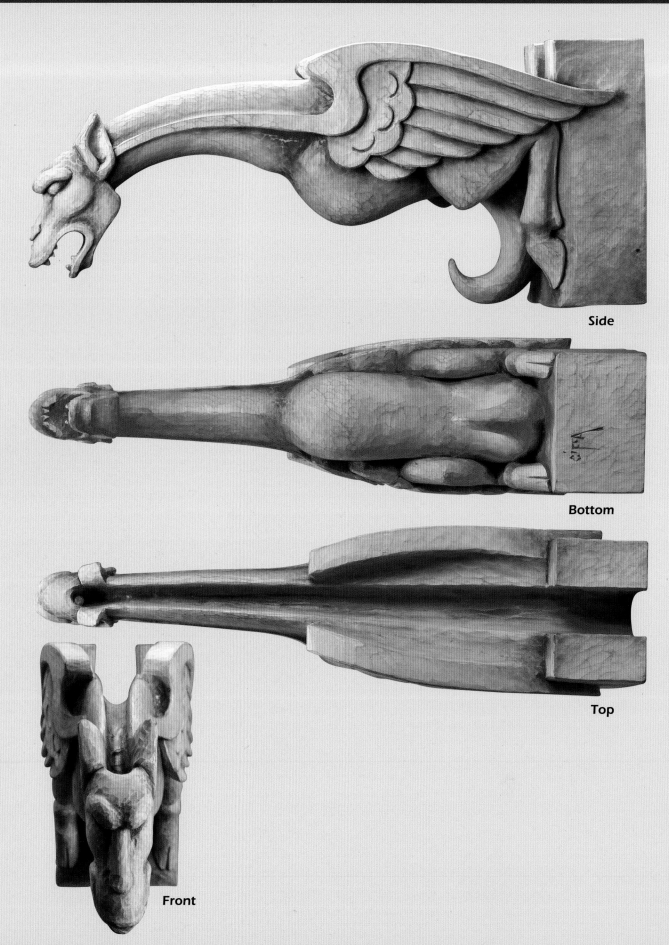

Side

Bottom

Top

Front

Lore

As mentioned in Part 1, the gargoyle's primary function was to divert rainwater from the roof away from the outer walls to prevent erosion. The most functionally effective way was to extend the gargoyle spout far away from the wall. This enabled the mason to combine form with function and design wonderfully horrendous creatures with long necks.

There is a French legend from around 600 AD that explains the gargoyle's name, physical form, and water spouting.

Outside the French town of Rouen dwelt a fire-breathing dragon named La Gargouille. La Gargouille was a typical monstrous dragon, sporting a long neck, powerful long jaws, and bat-like wings. It terrorized the townsfolk by devouring whole ships (and people), setting the city aflame, and spouting torrents of water that would cause flooding. Live human sacrifice was offered to the dragon, usually in the form of a criminal, but La Gargouille preferred maidens. Unfortunately, this offering did little to minimize the destruction.

A priest named Romanus, looking to convert people to Christianity, visited Rouen. The villagers agreed to build Romanus a church if he took care of the pesky dragon. The priest met La Gargouille and managed to subdue the monster with a crucifix. He led the now docile dragon back to town by means of a leash fashioned from his robe. The townsfolk immediately burned the dragon, but the head and neck would not burn. They had been tempered by La Gargouille's fiery breath.

The villagers decided to mount the head and neck upon the wall of the newly built church, as a reminder to all of St. Romanus' (and God's) power.

Artist Approach

Band saw the side pattern first. Next, taper the neck area to save some time in removing waste (refer to the image in Step 2 as reference). The top and bottom patterns are provided as visual reference.

I mounted the blank onto a plate accessory of my carving vise. This is the most advantageous set-up. I suggest you do the same, or something similar. If you do not own a similar vise system, mount a 2" x 4" (5cm x 10.2cm) block onto the base of the blank with large screws. This way, you can clamp the block into a conventional vise. The water channel running the length of the gargoyle is optional. However, I think it is a good study on how gargoyles actually functioned, so I have included it in the carving steps.

The finishing process is unconventional: linseed oil, artist oil paints, acrylic, and polyurethane. Yes, I know, it sounds strange, but it turns out quite well, and simulates a worn-stone look.

Install an inset keyhole-style hanger on the back. Sharpen your tools, take your time, and have fun.

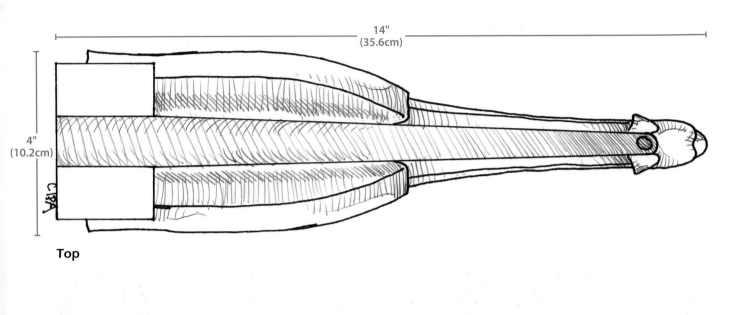

14"
(35.6cm)

4"
(10.2cm)

Top

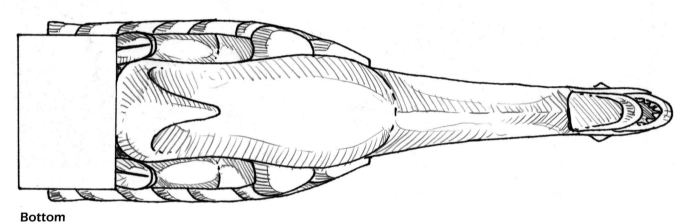

Bottom

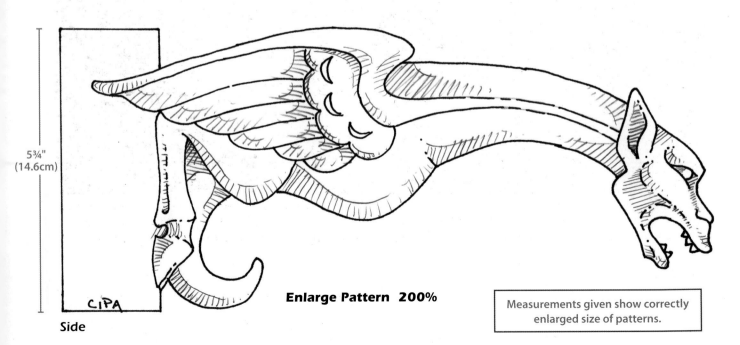

5¾"
(14.6cm)

Enlarge Pattern 200%

Measurements given show correctly
enlarged size of patterns.

Side

Tools and Materials List

- Basswood block 14" x 6" x 4" (35.6cm x 15.3cm x 10.2cm)
- ½" (12mm) V-tool
- Standard carving knife
- ¾" (20mm) Fishtail gouge
- ¼" (6mm) Half-round gouge
- ½" (12mm) Half-round gouge
- ⅛" (3mm) Veiner
- ⅛" (3mm) V-tool

- Detail knife
- ¼" (6mm) Shallow gouge
- Mallet
- Vise or clamping system of your choice
- Pencil/fine-tip permanent marker
- 14" (35.6cm) Band saw

Prepare the blank

With the side pattern drawn onto the 14" x 6" x 4" (35.6cm x 15.3cm x 10.2cm) block, start band sawing. Make relief cuts before sawing the outlines.

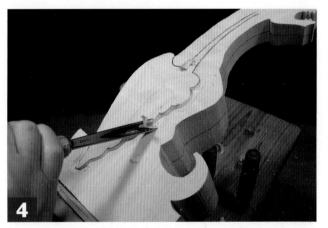

The blank is ready to go. Notice both top and side angles have been cut on the mounting block. Be sure to find and mark centerlines around the whole blank.

Define the wings

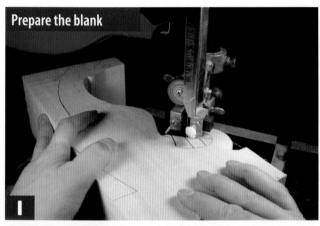

Due to the size of the carving, you will need to use a clamping/vise system of your choosing. I am using a self-made carving bench here, combined with a store-bought carving clamp (see page 155). Referring to the pattern, draw in the wing.

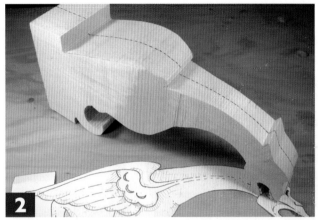

Because the wings are the outermost points, we must define them first. Use a ½" (12mm) or similar sized V-tool to separate the wing from the body. Using a mallet will give you more control. Expose about ¼" (6mm) of the wing's depth.

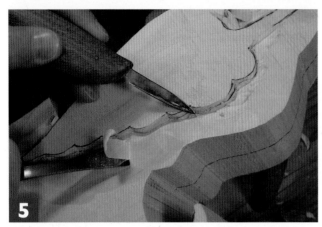

5

Use a carving knife of your choice to further define and clean up your V-cut. Use a ¾" (20mm) fishtail gouge to help remove waste outside the wing.

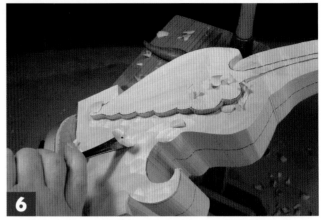

6

Using the ¾" (20mm) fishtail, continue to remove a uniform ¼" (6mm) of waste from around the wing, including the base. The idea here is to get to the next level. Do not remove any material in the neck area at this time, just let it taper off.

The area is leveled off ¼" (6mm) below the original surface, and the leg is drawn in.

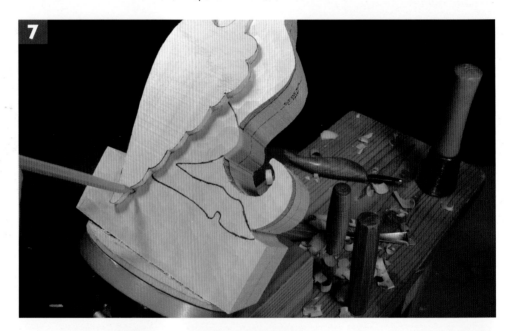

7

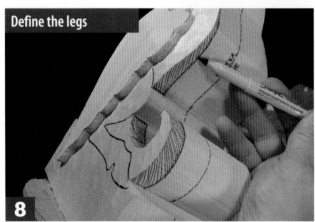

Define the legs

8

The leg will be ½" (12mm) thick, so another level must be removed in order to define it. This photo shows the area to be removed, as indicated by the hash marks. Notice how it tapers into the neck.

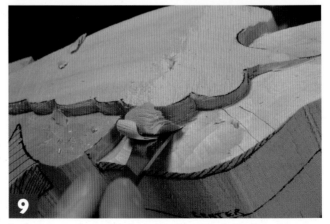

9

Begin to remove the waste in front of the knee. This may be done with a combination of the ½" (12mm) V-tool, the ¾" (20mm) fishtail, and the knife.

Notice that ½" (12mm) of waste has been removed, revealing the knee. I have undercut the wing a little.

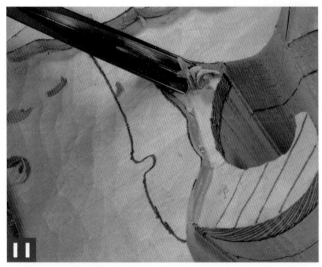

Now do the same with the area between the foreleg and hind leg/hoof area. Begin outlining with the ½" (12mm) V-tool...

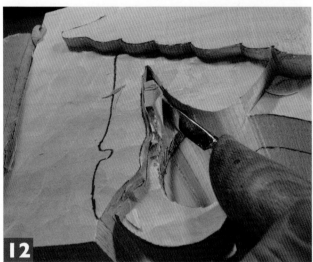

...and finish up with the knife and ¾" (20mm) fishtail. The knife is best for the tight area (as shown), and the fishtail will take care of the tail area. **Do not** undercut this area.

The leg is revealed. Notice the back of the hind leg and the base remain untouched.

Head and neck

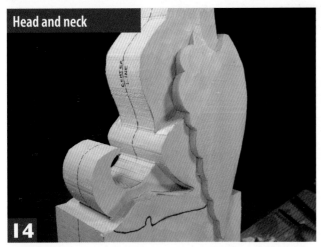

14

Turn the piece over and repeat Steps 3 through 13. The photo shows the left side in completion. This is a good time to compare each side to make sure the proportions are correct. When viewing from underneath...

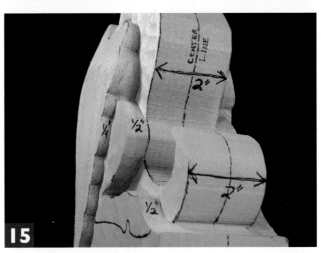

15

...the measurements should read as shown: the body at 2" (5cm) wide, the legs at ½" (12mm) wide, and the wings further back at ¼" (6mm) thick. This is why the presence of the centerline is important. Take a moment to study the photograph.

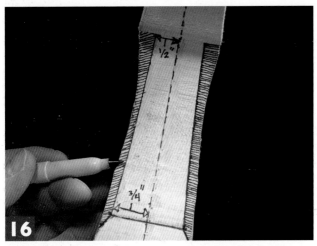

16

Next, carve the head and neck. From underneath, draw in guidelines as shown. From the jaw line to the base of the neck, the line should taper from ½" (12mm) (from the centerline), to ¾" (20mm).

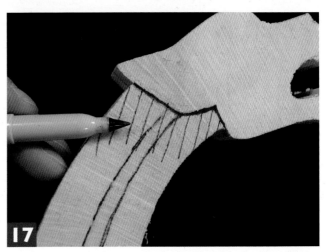

17

Now draw in the back of the ear on each side. (The right side is shown.) Refer to the pattern for correct placement.

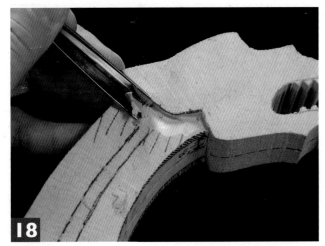

18

Using the ½" (12mm) V-tool, define the separation of head and neck, as shown. Do both sides.

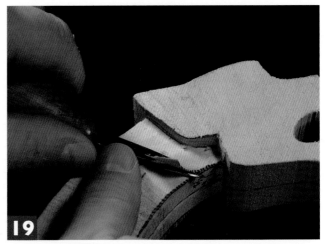

19

Using your knife, clean up the separation by way of stop cuts. Take it to the proper depth as defined by the guidelines underneath. Do both sides.

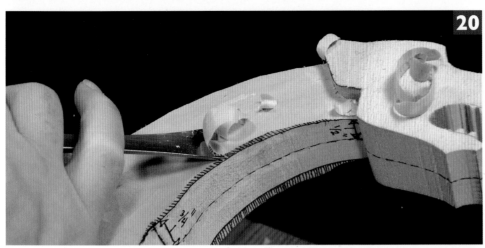

20 Using the ¾" (20mm) fishtail, taper the whole neck according to the guidelines. Be sure to keep the surface flat and even. Do both sides.

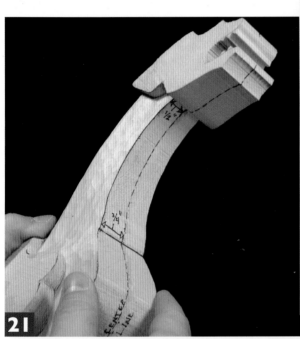

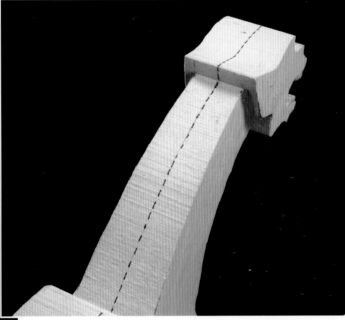

The neck has been tapered.

Detail the wings

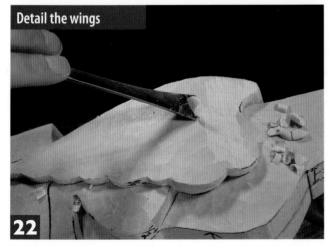

22

Now that the carving is mostly blocked out, we can pay attention to some details. Wings first: using the ¾" (20mm) fishtail, skim the top surface to erase the saw marks and even out the taper toward the neck. (The right wing is shown.)

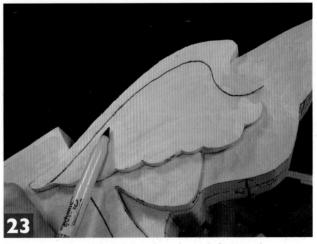

23

The wing is now tapered evenly into the neck area. Referring to the pattern, draw in the spine of the wing as shown.

24

Using the ½" (12mm) V-tool, I have trenched out material on the inner side of the spine. Do this by tilting the V-tool toward the inner side while cutting. Keep it shallow—about ⅛" (3mm). Perform the cut as cleanly as possible, taking several passes if required.

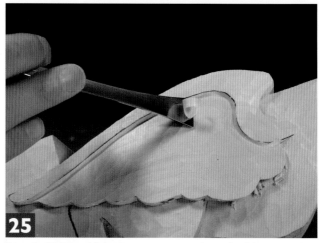

25

Using the ¾" (20mm) fishtail, remove waste on the inside of the cut in order to even out the V-cut.

26

Referring to the pattern, draw in the upper layer of feathers. As with the spine, use the tilted ½" (12mm) V-tool to define as shown. Again, only go ⅛" (3mm) deep. The knife can help to clean up the inner corners.

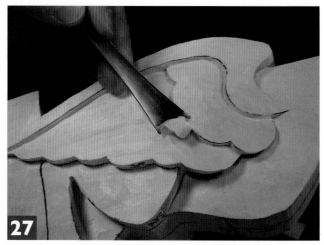

27

As before, use the ¾" (20mm) fishtail to even out the V-cut.

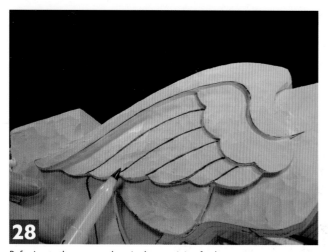

28

Referring to the pattern, draw in the remaining feathers.

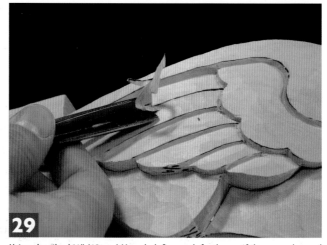

29

Using the tilted ½" (12mm) V-tool, define each feather as if they were layered on top of each other, as shown.

30 Use the ¾" (20mm) fishtail to smooth out each V-cut. Also, use the knife to clean up the corners and intersections where the lower and upper layers meet. (Both tools are shown to illustrate my point.)

31 This next detail is a small stylistic element. Draw in the crescents as shown, and carve them in with the ½" (12mm) V-tool. This should be performed in one clean action.

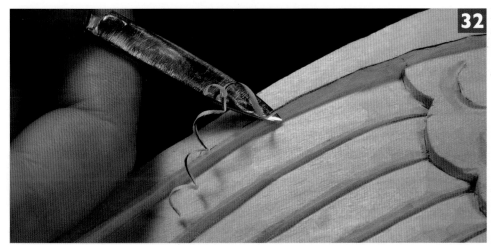

32 The final detailing is to clean up all hard edges by applying a very small bevel with the knife, as shown.

33 The finished wing. Repeat Steps 22 through 32 on the other side to complete the left wing.

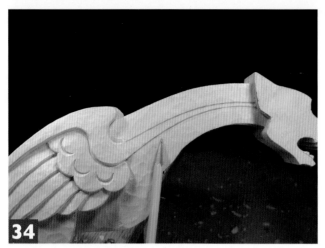

34 Next: On to the neck and body area. Referring to the pattern, draw in the stylized linear design along the length of the neck. It should run smoothly and gracefully from the spine of the wing. Use a pencil instead of a marker so you can erase what you don't remove.

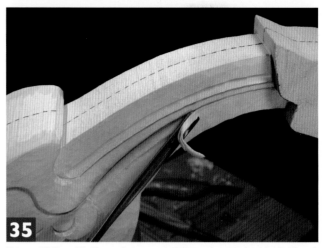

35 Using a ¼" (6mm) half-round gouge, carefully carve a trench on both sides of the linear design. Be sure to follow the lines smoothly and leave a crisp edge.

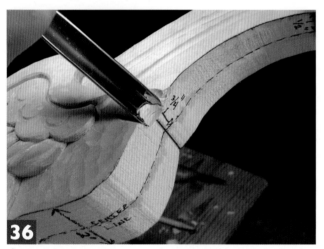

36 Using a ½" (12mm) half-round gouge, carve a trench, as shown, from the lower front corner of the wing to the center line underneath at the base of the neck.

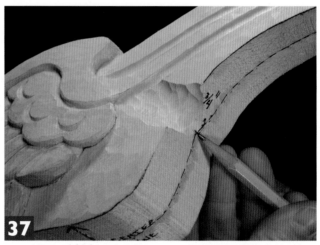

37 As you can see, I have taken several bites from the ¼" (6mm) trench to the centerline underneath to get through the hard corner.

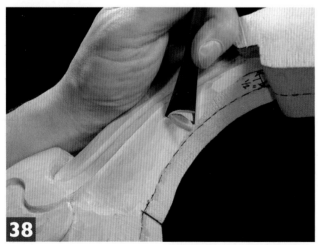

38 Using the ¾" (20mm) fishtail, begin to round this lower quarter of the neck, ending at the bottom centerline. Notice that I have left the stylized linear design intact.

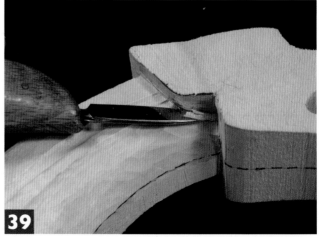

39 Make stop cuts with your knife to clean up the area where the neck joins the head.

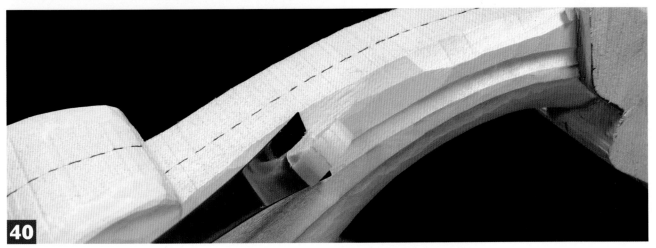

40 Now we round off the upper quarter of the neck as we did with the lower, except we aren't going all the way to the center mark. Carve just enough to smoothly round-over the hard edge. The top must remain flat for the water channel.

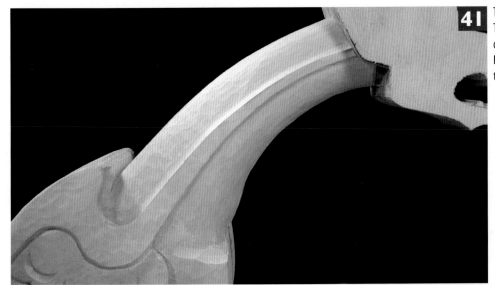

41 The right side of the neck is complete. The finished effect shows the linear design raised up from the surface. Repeat Steps 34 through 40 to finish the left side.

Detail the body

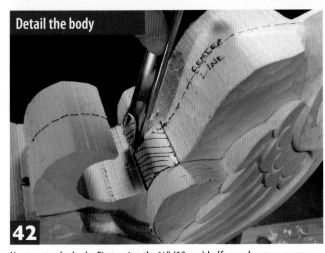

42 Next: on to the body. First, using the ½" (12mm) half-round gouge, remove the extra hump of waste wood on the underside between the knees.

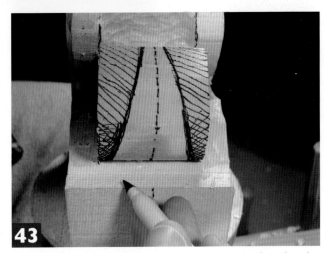

43 Draw the pointed tail underneath, as shown. We are going to shape the tail, and at the same time separate it from the hoof and legs.

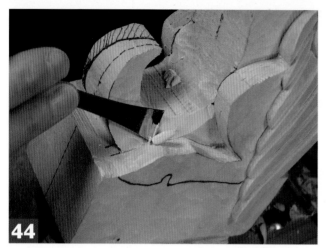

44 Proceed to remove the waste from the tail with the ¾" (20mm) fishtail. Remove what you can without marring the hoof or knee. Do both sides.

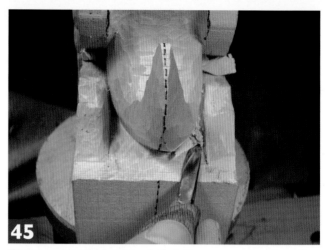

45 This step is a bit difficult. Using only the knife, remove waste between the hoof and tail while shaping the tail as you go. Here, I've completed the left side already for comparison. Take your time, use stop cuts, and take small bites.

46 The tail is fully formed, and the lower-leg sections are now defined as well.

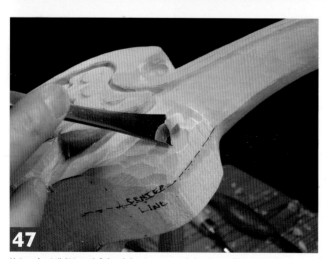

47 Using the ¾" (20mm) fishtail, begin to round the chest. Blend the chest smoothly into the already finished neck. The knife is also good for this task.

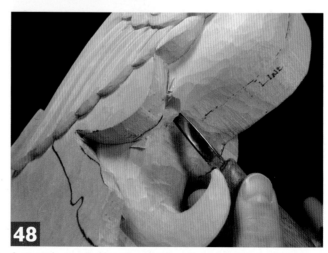

48 Continue the rounding from the chest down through the tail. Use the knife to help separate the knee from the underbelly. Repeat Steps 47 and 48 to complete the other side. Utilize the centerline as a point of reference in order to keep the overall shape balanced.

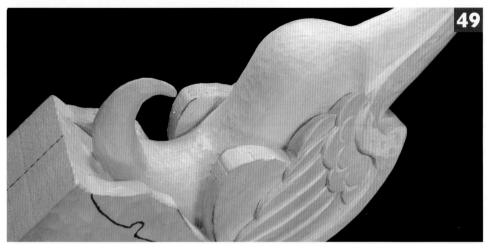

49 The body and tail have been completed. It's important to smoothly blend each section into the other. The result is one streamlined piece from the tip of the tail all the way up the neck.

Shape the legs

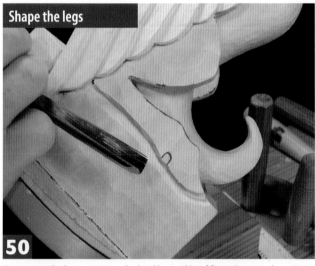

50 Next, on to the legs: separate the hind leg and hoof from the stone base. I have used the ½" (12mm) V-tool for this, skipping over the pastern (the gap between the fetlock and hoof). Cut only about ⅛" (3mm) deep, and remove as little of the base as possible.

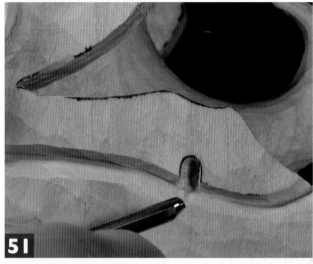

51 Using an ⅛" (3mm) veiner, hollow out the pastern as shown. Keep it clean, and go a little deeper than the V-cut.

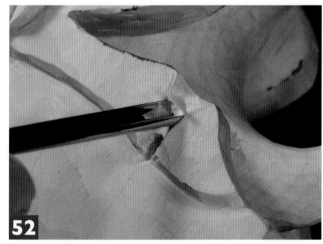

52 Using the ¼" (5mm) half-round gouge, hollow out and round the pastern joint, which helps to define the fetlock and the hoof.

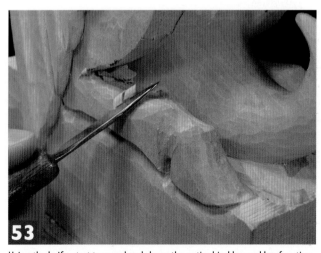

53 Using the knife, start to round and shape the entire hind leg and hoof section.

45

Once the hind leg and hoof are shaped, use the ¼" (6mm) half-round gouge to create the indentation of the rear tendon. Carve from the knob on the fetlock all the way to the back heel, as shown.

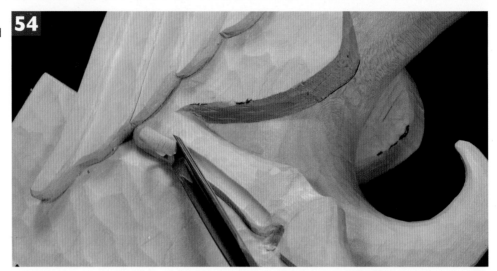

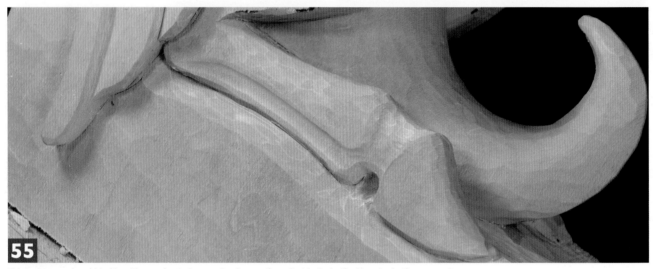

This is the completed hind leg. The tendon indent cut has been softened with the knife. Also, the knife was used to define the heel where it disappears behind the wing. Notice that the base material has been minimally removed—just enough to reveal the hind leg.

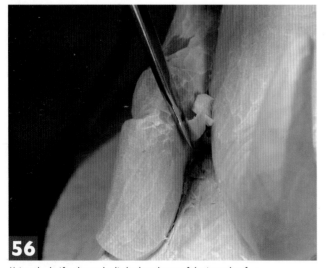

Using the knife, shape the little that shows of the inner hoof.

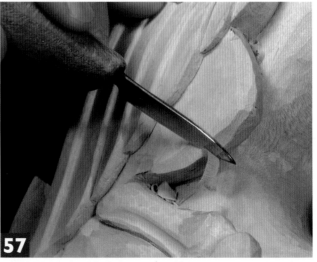

Using the knife, round the foreleg and knee section. This is a relatively simple action. Be sure to round the inner side as well.

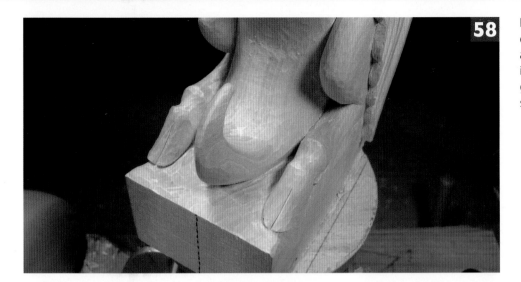

58

Repeat Steps 50 through 57 to complete the other leg. Here, both are shown complete. The final detail is to make the hooves cloven like a goat's—simply carve small vertical slits with the knife.

Detail the head

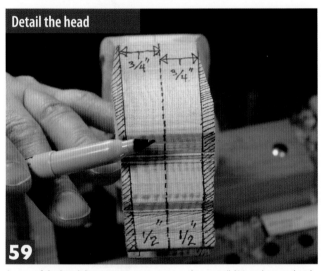

59

On top of the head, lay out measurements as shown: ¾" (20mm) on each side of the centerline at the tip of the ears, and ½" (12mm) on each side of the centerline down at the snout.

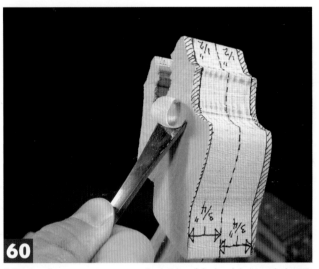

60

Following the measurements, taper both sides of the head down with the ¾" (20mm) fishtail.

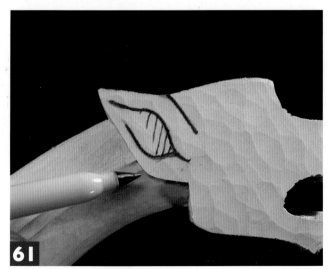

61

Once the head is at the proper width, draw in the right ear. Refer to the pattern for correct placement. Do both sides.

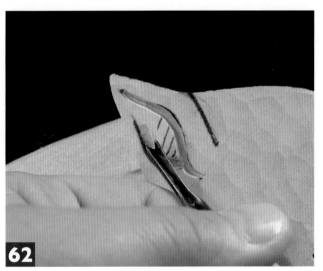

62

Using a ⅛" (3mm) V-tool, trace the lines of the inner ear, as shown. Do both sides.

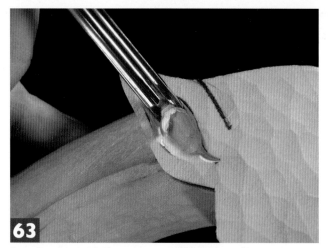

63

Using the ¼" (6mm) half-round gouge, hollow out the inner ear.
Do both sides.

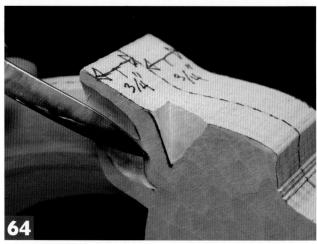

64

Using the knife, separate the ear from the top of the head by removing a
wedge of material, as shown. Do both sides.

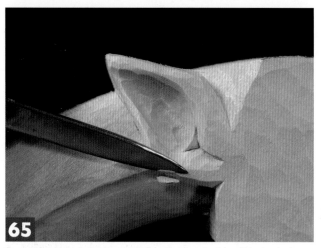

65

To complete the ear: Perform a final shaping by rounding off the hard edges
using the knife. Do both sides.

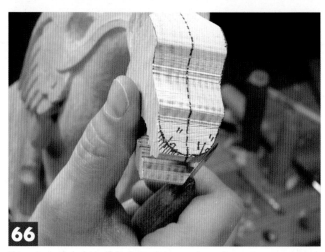

66

Using the knife, round off the front of the muzzle, as shown. Be sure to round
the lower jaw in alignment with the upper.

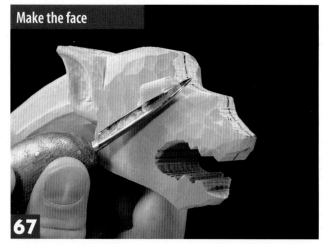

Make the face

67

Next: Start shaping the upper portion of the head with the knife by rounding
off the hard edges. Do both sides. Using the centerline as a guide, be sure to
shape each side equally.

68

The top of the head is in shape. Referring to the pattern, draw in the
bony brow line evenly across both sides. Be sure to re-define your
centerline as well.

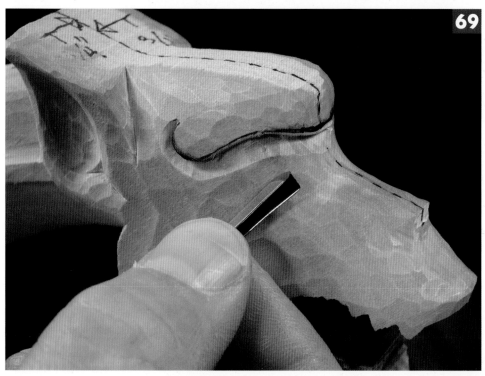

69 Using the ⅛" (3mm) V-tool, trace the brow line (with a tilt downward) as shown. Go all of the way around.

This birds-eye view shows how to define the nose bridge. We must remove material around it. Drawn-in guidelines are shown.

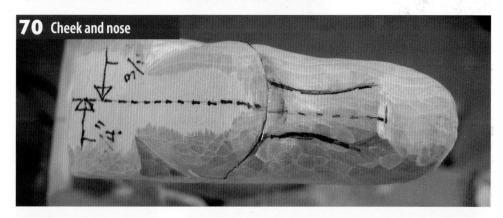

70 Cheek and nose

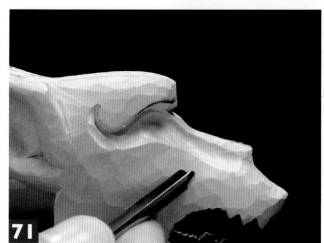

71

Using the ¼" (6mm) half-round gouge, scoop out waste along the lower side of the guideline. Follow through and hollow the eye socket area a bit.

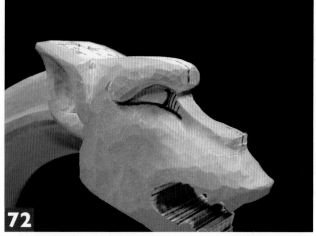

72

I have smoothed out the cheek a bit with the knife. Referring to the pattern, draw in the lower eyelid and the eyeball.

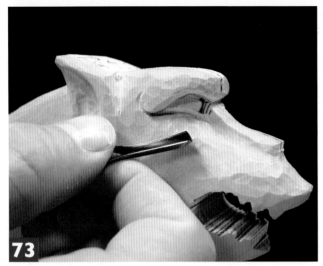

73

Trace the lower eyelid with the ⅛" (3mm) V-tool, as shown.

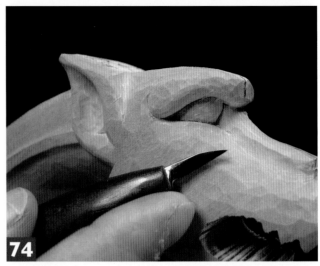

74

Using a detail knife, I have shaped the eyeball and smoothed out the bony brow. Repeat Steps 72 through 74 to complete the other eye. Be sure to match them up evenly.

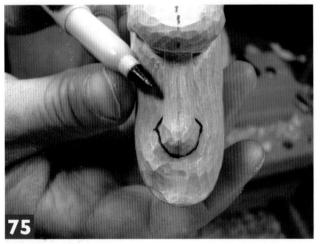

75

A bird's-eye view: Draw in the nose.

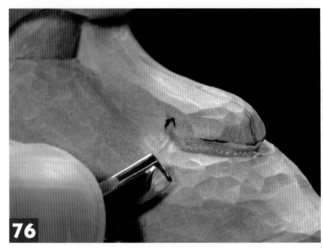

76

Trace the nose with the ⅛" (3mm) V-tool.

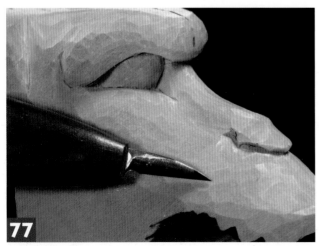

77

Here, the eyes and nose are complete, and the nose has been tweaked with the detail knife.

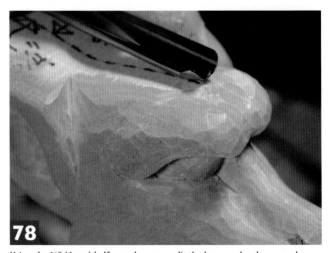

78

Using the ¼" (6mm) half-round gouge, split the brow and reshape, as shown.

Teeth, lips, and chin

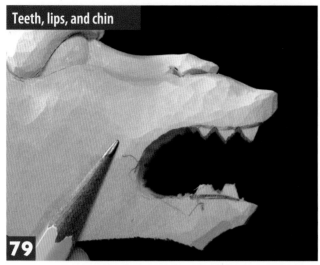

79 Draw in the separation of the teeth and lips. Do both sides.

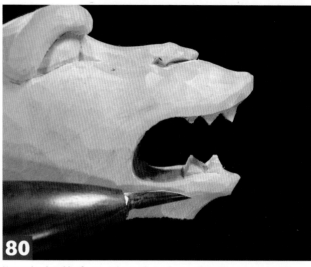

80 Using the detail knife, inset the teeth, as shown. Clean them up as well by removing the band saw marks. This takes a delicate touch—take care not to chip out the teeth or the edges of the lips. Do both sides.

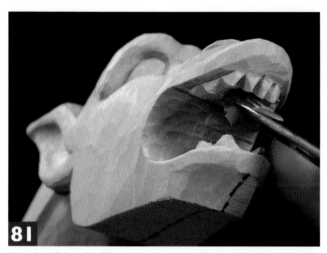

81 Using the ¼" (6mm) half-round gouge, remove the waste between the teeth inside the mouth. Also take this opportunity to clean up in the mouth, taking care not to damage the teeth.

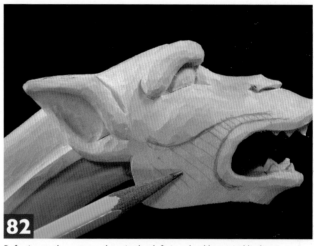

82 Referring to the pattern, draw in the defining cheekbone and lip lines, as shown.

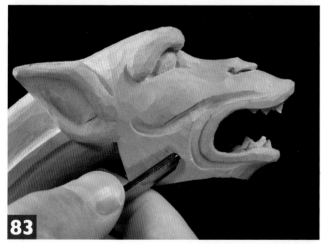

83 Using the ⅛" (3mm) veiner, trace the guidelines.

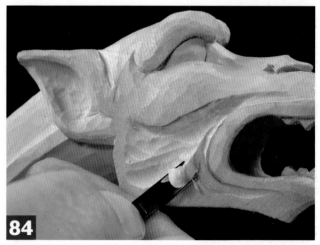

84 Using a ¼" (6mm) shallow gouge, slightly hollow the jowl area. This helps to define the cheekbone, jawbone, and mouth. Use this same tool to soften the hard veiner cut. Repeat Steps 82 through 84 to complete the other side.

The final step for the head is to clean up the saw marks underneath the lower jaw with the knife.

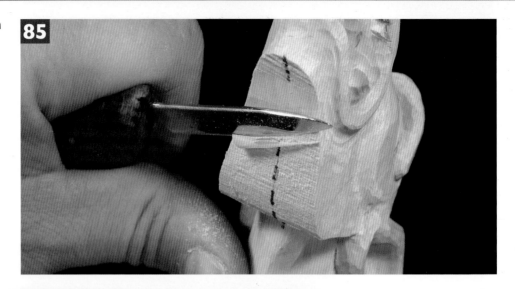

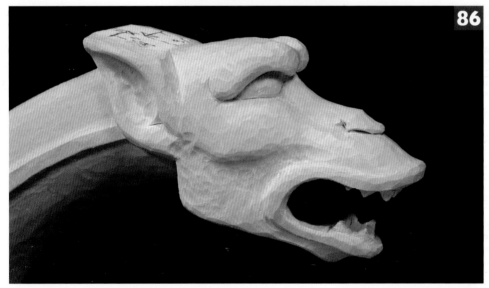

Here is the completed head. Now we clearly have a scary looking gargoyle.

Base and wings

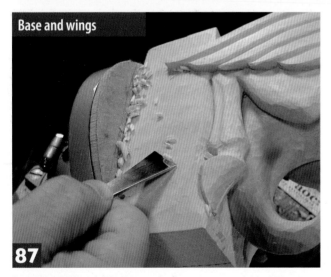

Using the ¾" (20mm) fishtail, erase the deeper gouge marks on the base as much as possible, leaving a finely tooled surface. Work all sides, as well as the top and bottom.

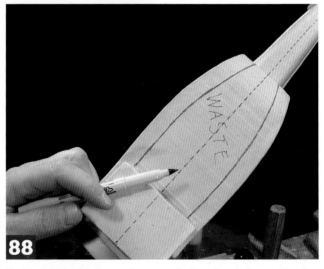

The last steps involve the top of our gargoyle. First, draw in the top edge of the wings—make them about ½" (12mm) thick.

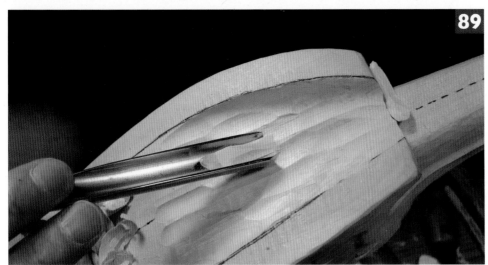

89 Using the ½" (12mm) half-round gouge, remove the waste between the wings. Don't go any deeper than the top surface of the neck.

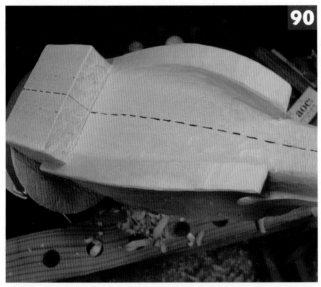

90 The area has been excavated, leveled, and cleaned up. I have re-drawn the centerline.

Note: If you do not wish to include a drain canal on your gargoyle, you may choose to stop at this point. If so, erase or remove any remaining lines, smooth out the top of the neck, separate the ears, and you are done.

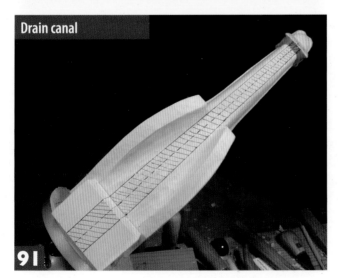

Drain canal

91 We will add the drain canal so water may travel the entire length of the carving and out of the mouth. Draw in guidelines so that the canal is 1" (2.5cm) wide at the base, narrowing to ½" (12mm) wide at the ears.

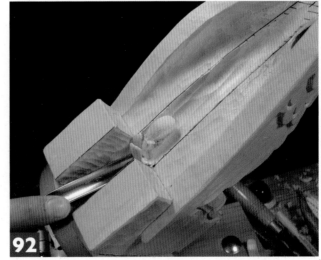

92 Start trenching out the canal, using the ½" (12mm) half-round gouge. This will require some effort, so take your time. The canal will have to be quite deep at the base, but it will only be ½" (12mm) deep along the neck.

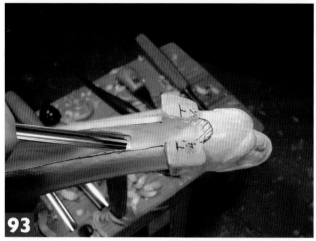

93 Switch to the ¼" (6mm) half-round gouge when hollowing up at the neck. Separate the ears; the trench will stop just ahead of them.

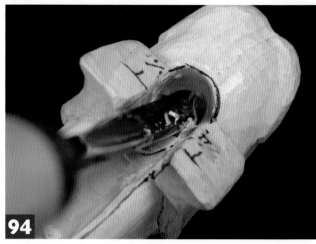

94 Between the ears, I have started to drill a hole with the ¼" (6mm) half-round gouge. To drill, push the gouge into the wood and turn it.

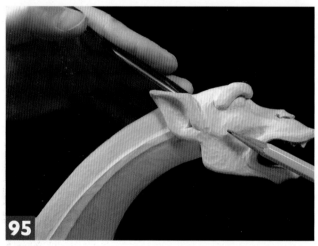

95 Carefully align the tool angle with the mouth, as if we were carving a throat. I prefer to use a hand tool instead of a power drill because it is a delicate operation.

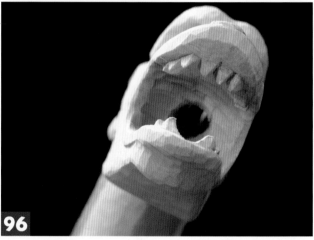

96 Here, I have broken through into the mouth. The passage is even round.

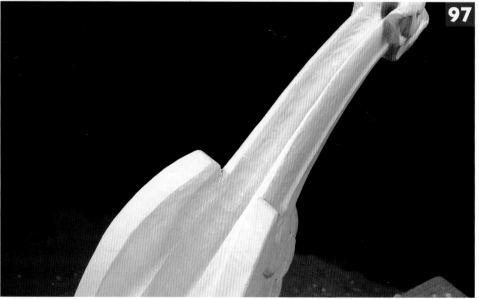

97 Clean up the overall trench and make it nice and smooth. Shape the tips of the ears a bit, and you are ready for finishing.

Finishing

The finishing process I developed uses linseed oil, artist oil paints, acrylic paints, and polyurethane. It simulates a worn-stone look quite well.

When creating your whitewash mixture, start with a portion of 50/50 linseed oil and mineral spirits blend—about a half-full baby food jar should be sufficient. Add a generous portion of white artist's oil color (comes in a tube). About a 3" (7.6cm) coil should be enough, but it may take experimentation to get the right strength. Seal the lid of the jar tightly and shake vigorously to mix the paint and oil. Apply the blend to a piece of scrap basswood until you get it to the strength you want.

When the finishing is complete and dried, install an inset keyhole-style hanger onto the back (be sure you have it centered), so your carving can be displayed on a vertical surface.

Tools and Materials List

- Disposable stain brush
- 50/50 mix of boiled linseed oil and mineral spirits
- Whitewash (mixture of linseed oil and mineral spirits blend and a generous portion of white artist oil color from tube)
- ¼" (6mm) round brush
- Medium-gray acrylic paint
- Rub-on satin polyurethane or regular polyurethane thinned with mineral spirits
- 0000 steel wool
- Latex gloves

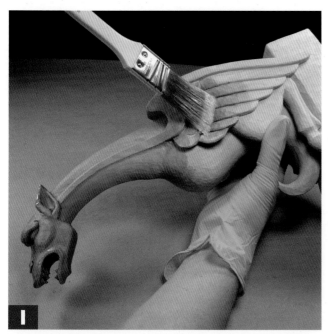

1 Using a disposable stain brush, liberally coat the entire carving with a 50/50 mix of boiled linseed oil and mineral spirits. Let it soak in for a few hours.

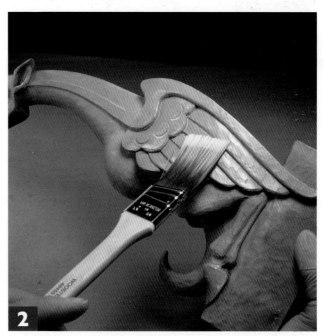

2 Liberally coat the entire carving with a whitewash mix of white artist oil color and the 50/50 linseed and mineral spirit solution (see the Finishing directions above). Work it in with the brush slowly and repeatedly. The oil in the whitewash solution will soak into the wood, progressively leaving more pigment on the surface.

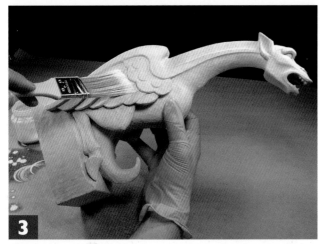

3

After several applications of the whitewash, the carving is appearing more white. Although it is difficult to see in photos, the white film is translucent. This is important—we do not want an opaque coating. Let the carving sit overnight to dry. Depending on how much whitewash was applied, it could take two nights before you can safely handle the gargoyle.

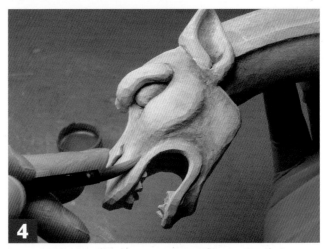

4

Using a ¼" (6mm) round brush, start to shade the deepened areas of the carving with medium-gray acrylic paint. Blend with water. This is an interpretive and freehand technique, so take your time and study the photos of the finished piece. Here I am working on the head area. I've applied paint to the corner of the eyes, the inside corner of the ears, and around the mouth.

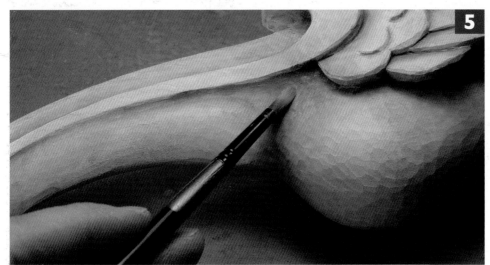

5

Apply the medium-gray paint to the neck and chest, especially the area between the neck and wing.

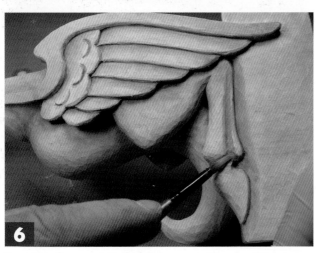

6

Concentrate the gray paint in the fetlock groove and the edge of the wings.

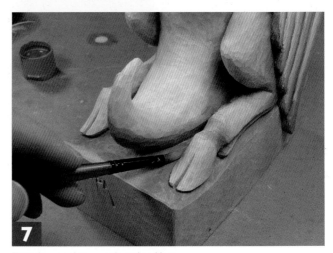

7

Paint the areas between the tail and legs.

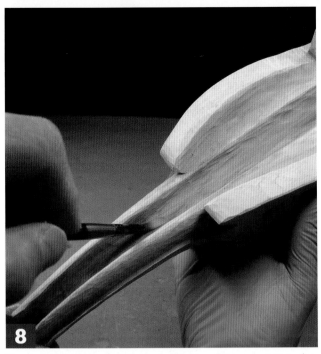

8

If you've added a water spout, the final application of the gray paint is to the channel on the top of the carving. Let the paint dry for a few hours.

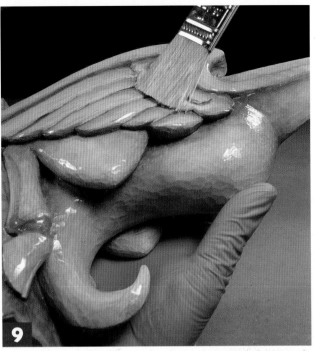

9

Apply a thin, but thorough, coat of mineral spirit—thinned satin or regular polyurethane over the entire carving. Apply one coat only; you will see that the whitewash will become more translucent as you apply the polyurethane. Let it dry overnight.

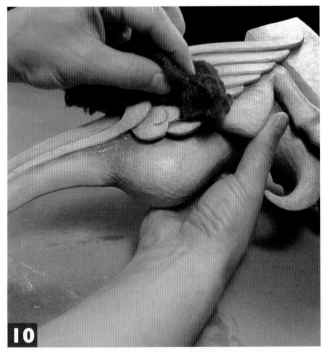

10

The final step is to buff the entire carving with 0000 steel wool. Be aggressive, so small areas and high points start to wear and the wood shows through. If successfully done, you will begin to see your tool marks from carving the surface of the wood.

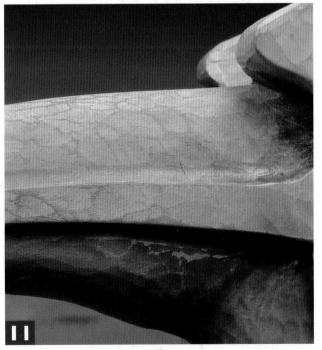

11

Shown is a close-up to illustrate my point: this is the desired effect. Take your time and go over the whole piece in this manner.

The Classic
Grotesque **Step-by-Step**

Our classic grotesque design has been developed with the many figures found at Paris' Cathedral of Notre-Dame in mind. The building has many non-functional grotesque figures peering down from the balconies above. This design has a bony hunched back, long pointed ears, muscular arms, and an almost humorous leer. This piece would be best displayed up high somewhere so the grotesque can look down upon his admirer, as he originally was meant to do.

Side

Front

Top

Back

Lore

The traditional grotesque image invokes descriptions such as ugly, weird, bizarre, distorted, and even absurd. By definition, the grotesque is a distortion of the natural. Grotesque art, in all of its forms, is never pretty. Whether it is painting, graphic design, or sculpture, grotesque art spans the centuries back to the most ancient forms of artistic expression. The oldest grotesque images originally were meant to tell stories, and to express the basest of human emotion. Ancient Greek mythology had grotesque characters: Medusa—the snake-haired Gorgon, the foul Harpies, and the bull-headed Minotaur are a few. The Pacific Northwest coastal Native American tribes carved large totem poles that depicted grotesque images of their animalistic ancestors. The Balinese carved grotesque masks in the image of Rangda, an evil widow witch of traditional lore. During the Middle Ages, medieval artists created countless images of underworld grotesquery in paintings and sculpture alike. Even today, we see modern grotesque images in motion pictures and political cartoons. The Mardi Gras parades in New Orleans and Rio de Janeiro sport grotesque imagery in the form of humorous and sometimes scary masks.

The classic grotesque figure also has been portrayed in literature. Mary Shelley's Frankenstein's monster and Victor Hugo's hunchback of Notre-Dame are both good examples of the tragic character: repulsive and vile to most, but with a tender side of humanity that strives to overcome cruel odds in life.

Close-up of fingers.

61

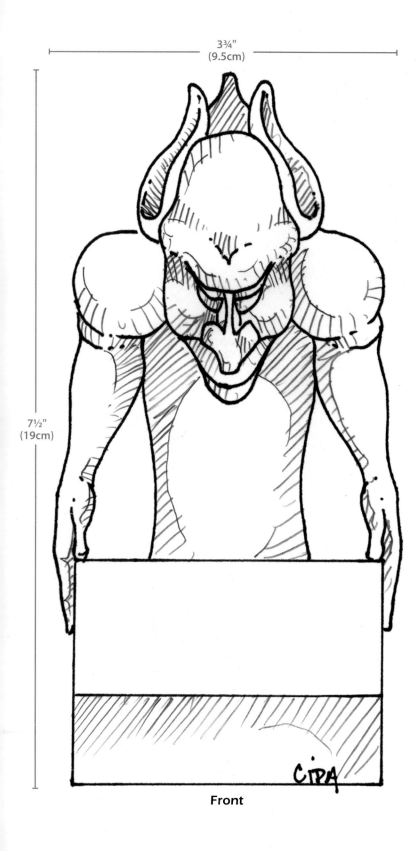

3¾"
(9.5cm)

7½"
(19cm)

Cipa

Front

Artist Approach

I decided to carve the grotesque from a butternut block measuring 8" x 5½" x 3¾" (20.3cm x 14cm x 9.5cm). The side-view pattern is used to band saw the blank, while the front and rear views are for reference only. I mounted the blank onto a plate that happens to be an accessory of my carving vise. This is the most advantageous set-up; I would suggest you do the same, or similar, if possible. If you do not own a similar vise system, mount a 2" x 4" (5cm x 10cm) block onto the base of the blank using large screws. This way, you can clamp it into a conventional vise by the block, eliminating the possibility of marring the actual carving.

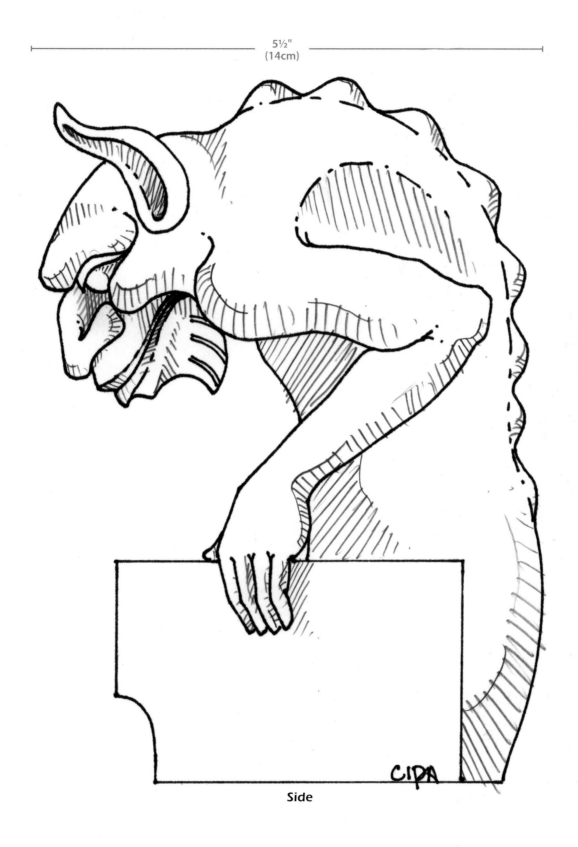

5½"
(14cm)

Side

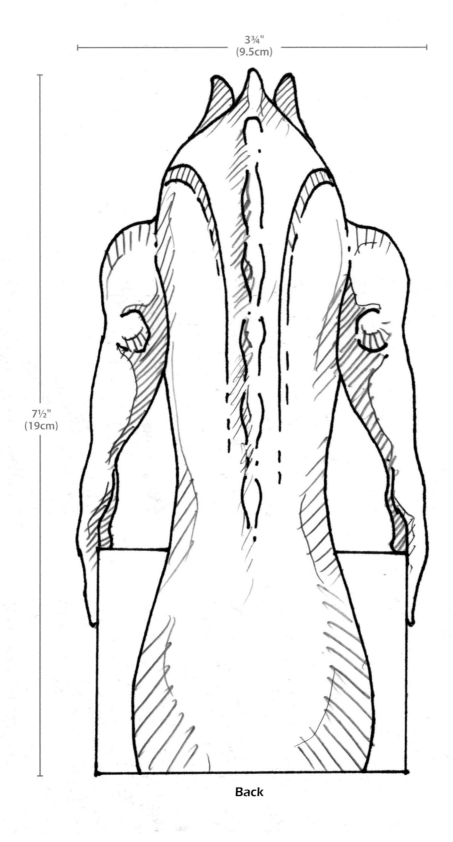

3¾"
(9.5cm)

7½"
(19cm)

Back

Tools and Materials List

- Butternut block 8" x 5½" x 3¾" (20.3cm x 14cm x 9.5cm)
- ½" (12mm) V-tool
- ¾" (20mm) Fishtail gouge
- ½" (12mm) Half-round gouge
- Small skew chisel (optional)
- Standard carving knife
- ¾" (20mm) Shallow gouge, or similar tool
- ¼" (6mm) Half-round gouge
- ¼" (6mm) Shallow gouge

- ½" (12mm) Fishtail gouge
- ⅛" (3mm) Veiner
- Detail knife
- ⅛" (3mm) V-tool
- Mallet
- Vise or clamping system of your choice
- Pencil or fine marker
- 14" (35.6cm) Band saw

The 8" x 5½" x 3¾" (20.3cm x 14cm x 9.5cm) butternut blank has been band sawed to shape using the side pattern. I have not sawed out other perspectives because it would be too easy to cut something vital off. Be sure to mark the all-important centerline, and mount the blank to your clamping device.

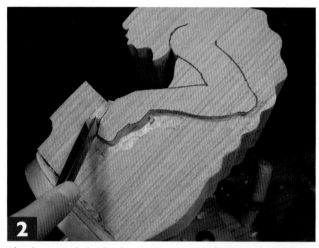

After drawing in the hand and arm section, start to define it using a ½" (12mm) V-tool. It is important to go no deeper than ¼" (6mm) around the hand gripping the base. Tilt the V-tool toward the waste side for more efficiency.

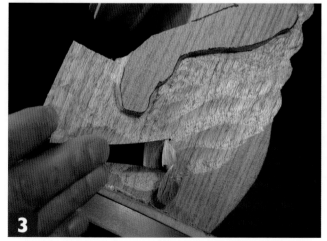

Using a ¾" (20mm) fishtail gouge, remove waste around the hand and arm section. Be sure to evenly remove wood no more than a ¼" (6mm) deep around the base area.

Once the area is evenly leveled, refer to the pattern and draw in the stone base as shown. The hash marks represent waste wood to be removed.

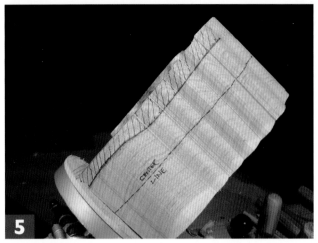

5 Before removing waste, set guidelines for the rear view. Referring to the pattern, draw in the contour of the hip and back line. Notice that we are only concerned with the left side at this point.

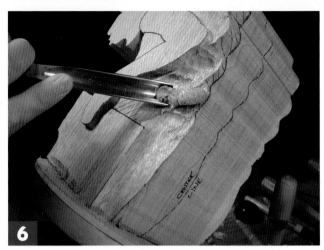

6 Remove waste with a ½" (12mm) half-round gouge. Begin with the area between the base and the forearm.

7 I have used the gouge to cleanly scoop out waste below the arm, using the V-cut created in Step 2 as a guide. Be sure not to undercut the arm or the base.

8 Before removing waste above the arm, look at the front view to define the width of the head. From the centerline, measure out 1¼" (3.2cm) at the tip of the ear, tapering to 1" (2.5cm) down at the tip of the nose.

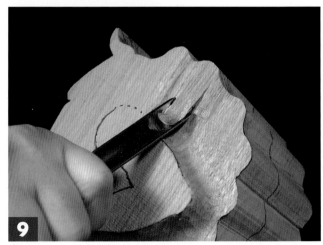

9 Using the ½" (12mm) half-round gouge, remove waste from the sides of the hunched back and work across toward the head.

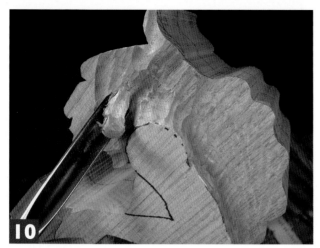

10 Remove waste from the head, working around the shoulder. Be mindful of the depth guidelines.

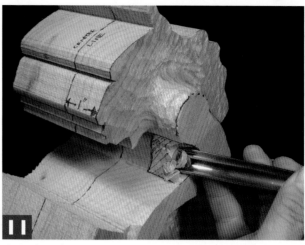

11 The head area has been cut to depth. Using the ½" (12mm) half-round gouge, clear out the small pocket of waste on the inside of the elbow. Go about 1" (2.5cm) deep, keeping in line with the rest of the body.

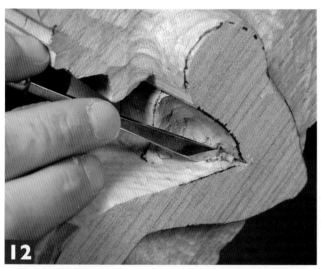

12 As shown, use a small skew chisel to clean out the inside corner the gouge cannot get. A knife will also work.

13 Use the skew chisel or knife to sharpen the inner corners of the base where the gouge cannot reach.

14 The hand and arm section clearly stands apart from the head and body section, as does the base. Repeat Steps 2 through 13 to complete the right side of the grotesque.

Shape the back

15 Using a ¾" (20mm) or similarly sized shallow gouge, begin to round and shape the back, starting from the bottom. Work your way up, as shown. Do not cross the centerline.

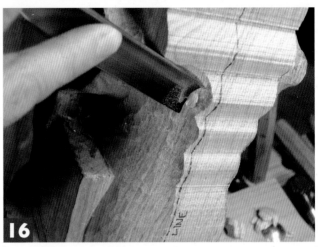

16 When carving close to the ridged spine, scallop out a hollow along the centerline in an attempt to form a raised backbone. We will refine it later.

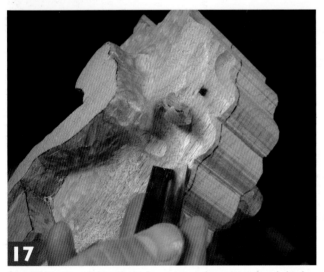

17 As you move upward along the back, you may undercut waste from behind the jutting elbow. We will refine it later when working on the arms.

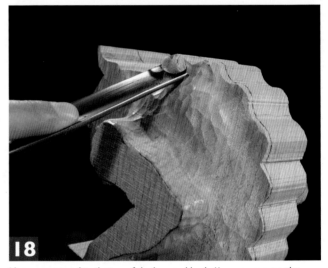

18 I have progressed to the top of the humped back. Here you can see the ridged spine is much more pronounced. Notice how I am scalloping along the ridge itself.

19 Switching to the ½" (12mm) half-round gouge, trench out a deeper depression to show the neck area behind the ears.

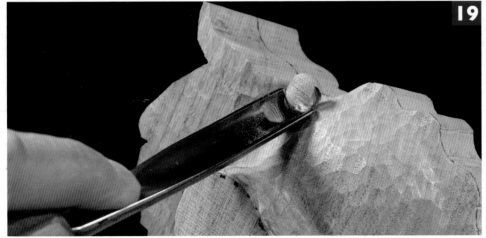

20

The entire back is roughed into shape. Repeat Steps 15 through 19 to complete the grotesque's right side.

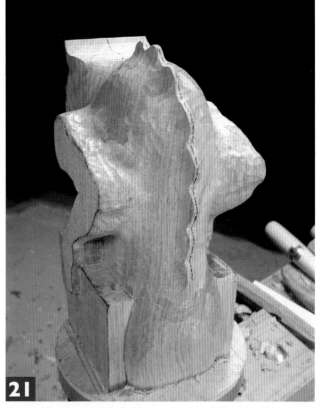

21

This rear view shows that both sides are now shaped. There should be a narrow waist, a humped back, and a raised, ridged spine from top to bottom.

Shape the arms

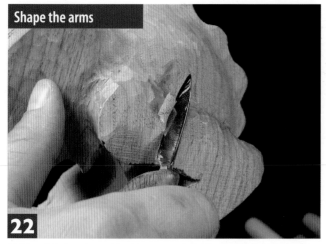

22

At this point, there is considerably more material than needed on the upper arms. Using a knife, begin to whittle down the excess. Maintain the muscle tone as you go.

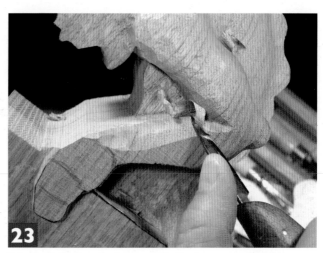

23

Using the knife, shape the forearm. Notice the deep crease where the inner elbow bends. Refer to the pattern and finished photos closely while shaping the arm. The elbow has taken on a knobby appearance as well.

24 Continue to shape the forearm. Remember to maintain the muscle tone. Define the bend in the wrist as well.

25 Create the wrist and general shape of the hand with the knife. As you can see, the hand itself has been modeled into three separate planes: the lower fingertips, the middle joints, and the back of the hand.

26 The grotesque's entire left arm is falling into shape. It still has not been hard-separated from the body; we have just defined the outer portion. Complete Steps 22 through 25 to bring the right arm up to speed.

Remove waste

27 Before we can complete the arms, the waste must be removed in between to expose the chest and abdominal area. The first stage of removal is marked out here.

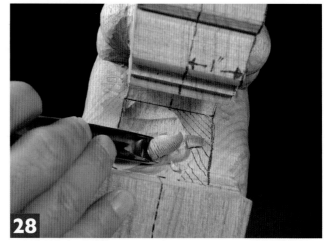

28 Using the ½" (12mm) half-round gouge, begin to remove the waste. Be aware of the abdominal contour as you go, and remember to maintain the flat plane of the base surface.

29 I have removed as much as I can with the ½" (12mm) gouge without compromising essential material. I went about 1¼" (3.2cm) deep, measured from the thumb tips planted on the base.

Shape the inner arms and waist

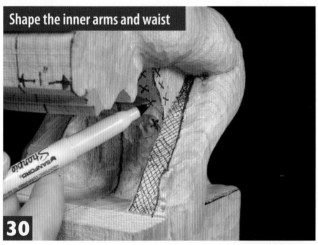

30

The next few steps are tricky, and require some thought before attempting. As shown, I have marked the inner profile of the left arm. As this is removed, the hard corner of the chest will need to be rounded, as indicated by the *X* marks.

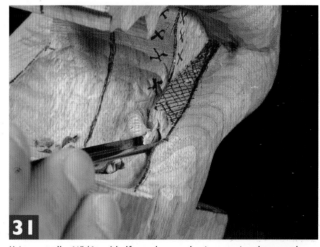

31

Using a smaller ¼" (6mm) half-round gouge, begin removing the waste by taking small, controlled bites. Be aware of the inner thumb profile as you go.

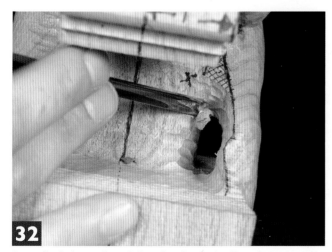

32

Eventually, the bites will punch through to the rear. It will now be progressively easier to remove more of the waist as the opening increases in size.

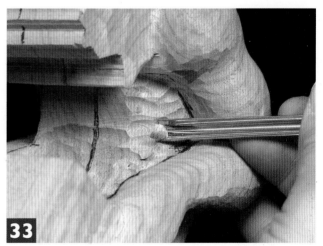

33

Moving upward, round the chest. Use your re-drawn centerline as a point of reference.

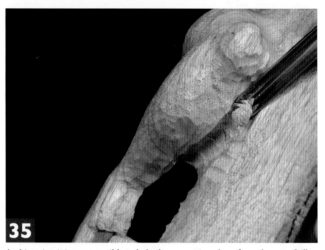

34 Continue plugging along. The profile of the waist is taking shape, and the arm is becoming more independent of the body.

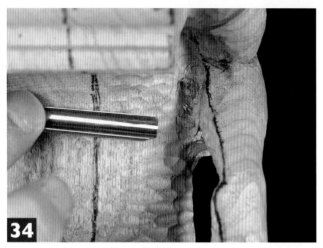

35 At this point, it is now possible to help the separation along from the rear. Still using the ¼" (6mm) gouge, deepen the trench between the elbow and body.

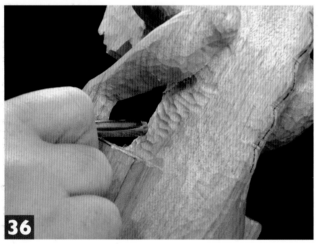

36 Continue to shape and round the waist with the ¼" (6mm) half-round gouge.

Define the arms

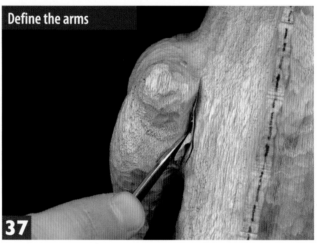

37 I have gone as far as the gouge can take me. Using the knife, I am continuing to define the separation of arm and body from the rear.

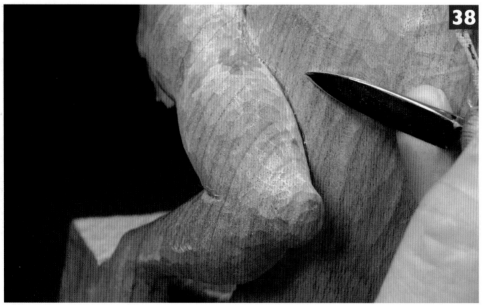

38 Using the knife, I have completely defined the separation of upper arm and back. I also have rounded the upper arm to its final form, as well as smoothing out the adjoining back area. Notice the elbow's knobby shape.

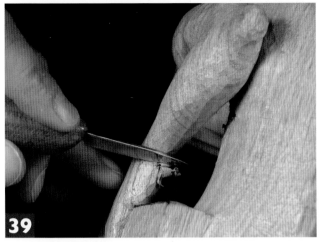

39

Still using the knife, round the back of the forearm into its final shape. Be sure to define the back of the wrist as well as the fleshy back of the hand. I also have smoothed out the gouge marks from the waist.

40

Moving to the front, shape the inner forearm. The wrist is in shape and the thumb is partially formed.

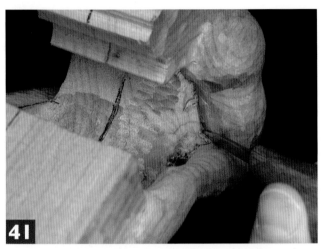

41

Using the knife, start to remove the waste up in the inner elbow and along the inner bicep area. This is a rather tight area, and will take patience to remove.

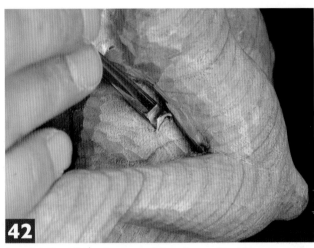

42

A small shallow ¼" (6mm) gouge can help to clean up this tricky area.

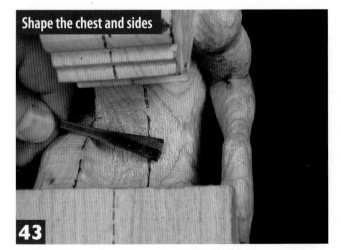

Shape the chest and sides

43

The left arm is complete. I have used a ½" (12mm) fishtail to smooth out the chest and abdominal area. Repeat Steps 30 through 43 to complete the right arm.

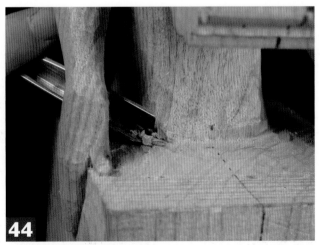

44

Using the ½" (12mm) V-tool, define a hard separation of the body from the base. Be sure to maintain the level surface of the base.

45

Using a ½" (12mm) fishtail, clean up the V-cut around the torso.

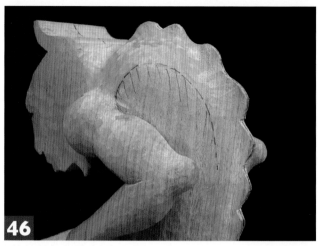

46

Add this stylized detail. Refer to the pattern and draw in the guideline for this bony feature as shown.

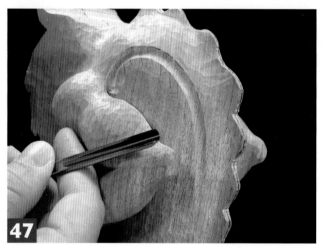

47

Using the ¼" (6mm) half-round gouge, I have traced a groove along the inside of the guideline. Be sure it tapers off smoothly down along the spine.

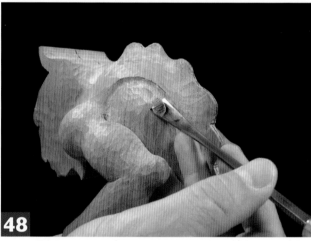

48

Using the ½" (12mm) fishtail, smooth the hard edge left by the gouge on the inside of the cut only. Leave the hard edge on the outside. Erase any marker or pencil marks with the knife, if required.

Notice the overall effect. The humped roundness of the hunched back has been maintained. Also, notice how the groove runs smoothly from the back of the armpit. Repeat Steps 46 through 48 to complete the other side.

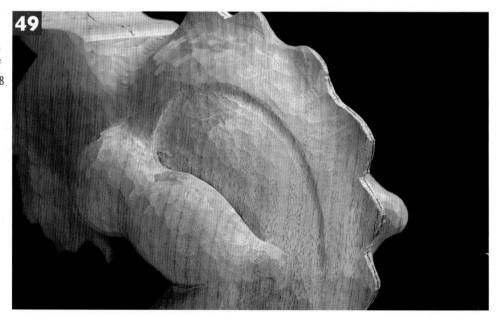

49

Detail the back and hands

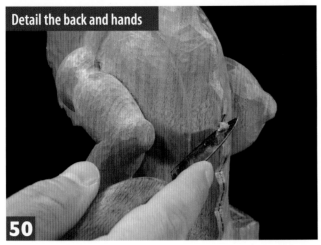

50

Using the knife, clean up the uncarved edges of the bony ridges along the spine.

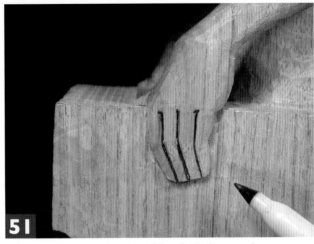

51

Referring to the pattern, draw in guidelines for the fingers as shown.

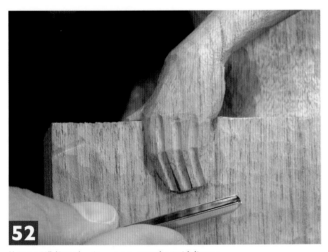

52

Using a ⅛" (3mm) veiner, trace over the guidelines.

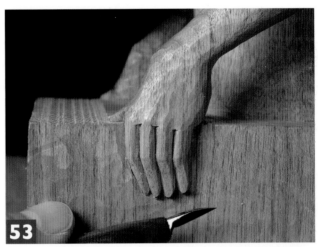

53

Using a small detail knife, I have defined the fingers by separating them. I have also shaped them into their final form. Notice the rounding of the fingertips.

54

Using the detail knife, I have defined the thumb by separating it from the hand, as shown.

55

A final hand detail: Draw in the inner profile of the thumb. Waste must be hollowed out in order to reveal the palm.

56

Using the ¼" (6mm) shallow gouge, hollow out the palm.

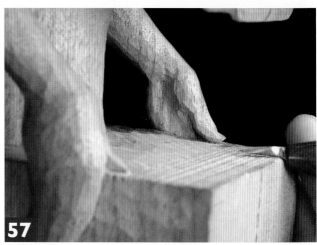

57

With the help of the detail knife to clean up, the inner palm and thumb area is complete. Repeat Steps 51 through 57 to complete the other hand.

Clean and level the base

58

Using the ½" (12mm) fishtail, clean up and level the base top into its final form.

59

Also clean and level the front and sides. Use the ½" (12mm) half-round gouge for the curved undercut, as shown.

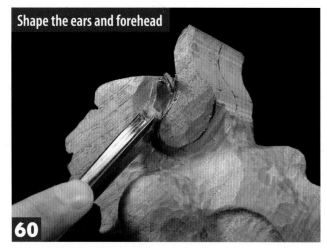

Shape the ears and forehead

60

We've saved the head for last. Referring to the pattern, draw in the ear and start to define it with the ½" (12mm) V-tool as shown. Do both sides.

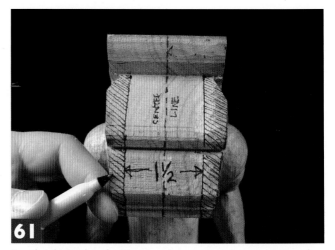

61

Now that the ears have been positioned, we must remove more waste and narrow the head to a total width of 1½" (3.8cm). Using the centerline as a guide, I have marked the material to be removed.

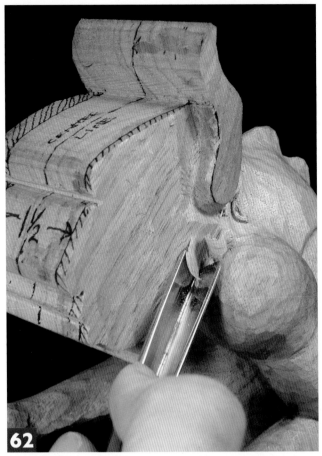

62 Start to remove the waste with the ¾" (20mm) fishtail (not shown), alternating with the ½" (12mm) V-tool to deepen the areas around the shoulder and ear. Do both sides.

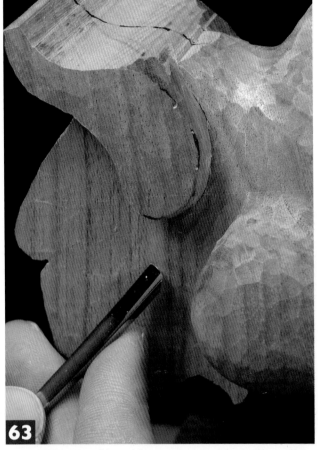

63 Notice the deepening of the neck between the ear and the shoulder, and how all three elements tie together. I have used the ¼" (6mm) shallow gouge to clean up in there.

64 Using the ¾" (20mm) fishtail, round out the forehead area. I have already completed the left side.

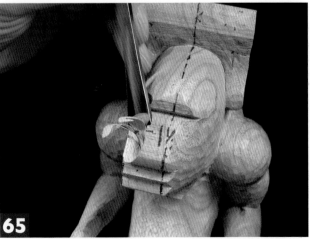

65 Still using the fishtail, taper the entire facial profile from the rear, working forward toward the centerline. As you can see, I have already completed the left side.

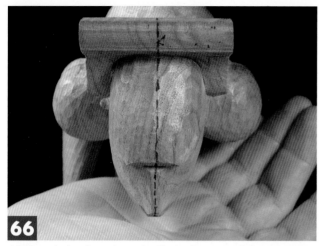

66 A high-angle shot shows the results. The face has essentially been shaped into a hatchet form.

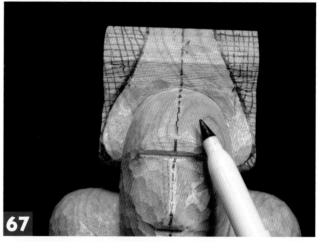

67 Now that the head is formed, the front profile of the ears can be refined. Shown are guidelines for waste removal.

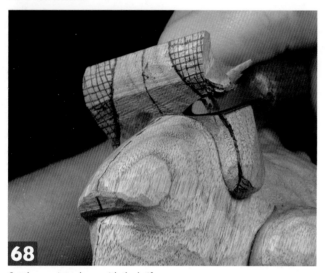

68 Get the ears into shape with the knife.

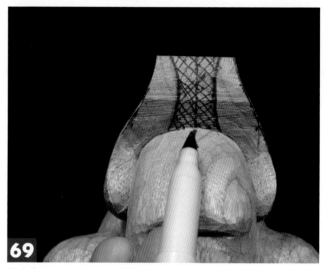

69 Mark the waste to be removed between the ears.

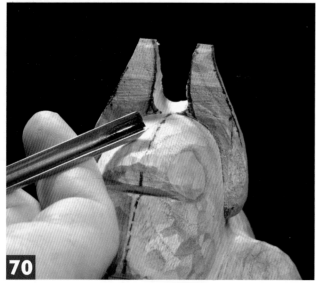

70 I have used the ¼" (6mm) half-round gouge to remove the waste. **Be careful:** Do not break off the tips of the ears!

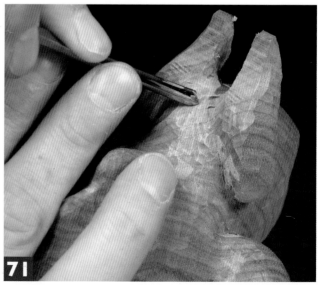

71 Using the ¼" (6mm) shallow gouge, clean up the top of the head behind and between the ears.

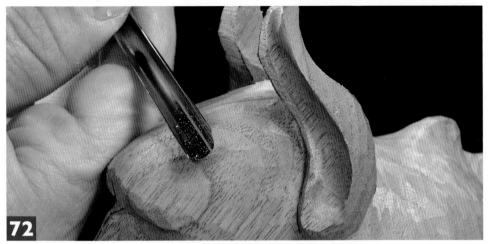

72 Using the ¼" (6mm) half-round gouge, I have hollowed out the left ear, as shown. Perform this action cleanly and smoothly. Do the other ear.

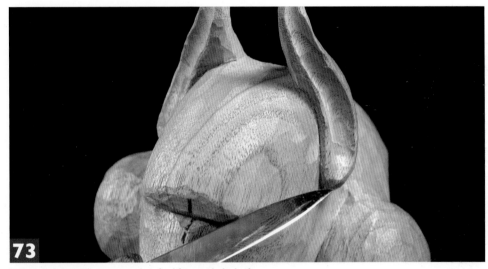

73 Hollow and shape the ears into their final form with the knife.

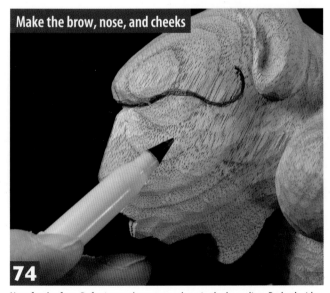

Make the brow, nose, and cheeks

74 Now for the face. Referring to the pattern, draw in the brow line. Do both sides.

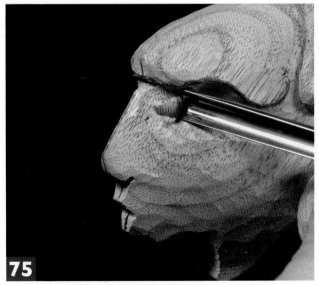

75 Using the ¼" (6mm) half-round gouge, hollow the eye socket area while using the brow line as a guide. Do both sides.

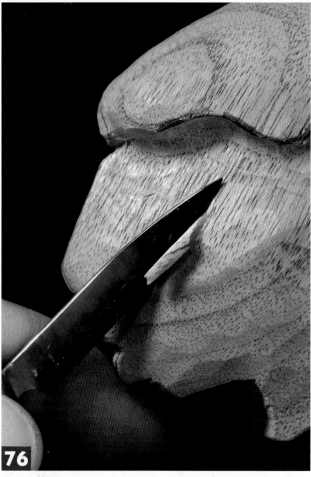

76

Using the knife, smooth out the gouge marks on the cheek surface. Do both sides.

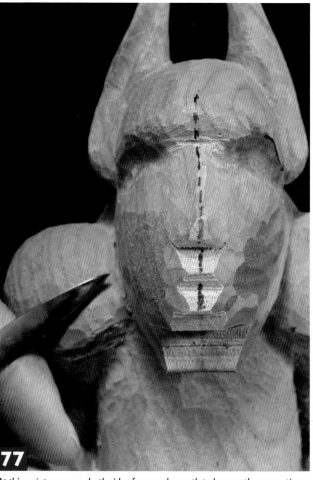

77

At this point, compare both sides from underneath to be sure the proportions are correct. Tweak with the knife if needed.

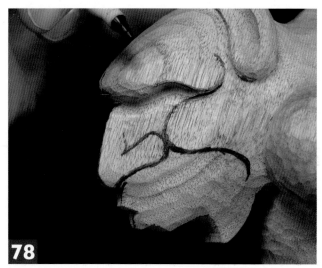

78

Referring to the pattern, draw in the cheek and nose, as shown. Do both sides, and be sure to align each side carefully when drawing.

79

Using a ⅛" (3mm) V-tool, I have defined the cheek and nose by tracing the lines, as shown. Be sure to carve up into the brow line as well. Do both sides.

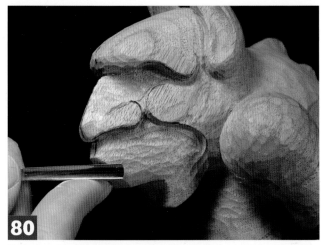

80

Using the ¼" (6mm) shallow gouge, I have smoothed out the V-cuts below the cheek line by tapering towards the front centerline. I have also smoothed out the eye socket area. Do the other side.

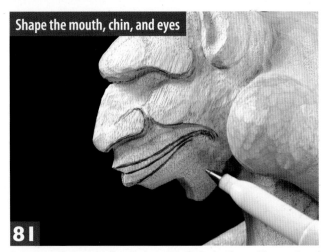

Shape the mouth, chin, and eyes

81

Referring to the pattern, draw in the mouth. Do both sides, and be sure they are symmetrical.

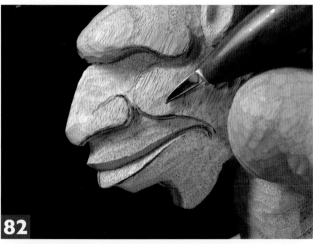

82

Using a detail knife, carve in the mouth. This is a simple operation, only requiring an applied V-cut. Be sure to keep it smooth and controlled when cutting. Do the other side.

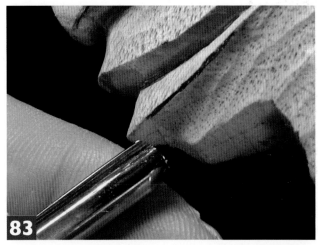

83

Using the ¼" (6mm) half-round gouge, scallop up underneath the bottom lip. This action helps to define the mouth. Do the other side.

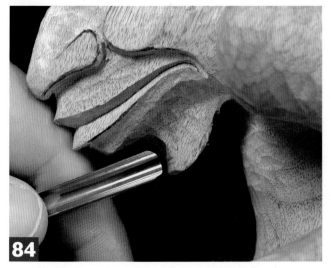

84

Using the ¼" (6mm) half-round gouge, define the chin from the beard by deeply scalloping out material below the chin line. Do the other side.

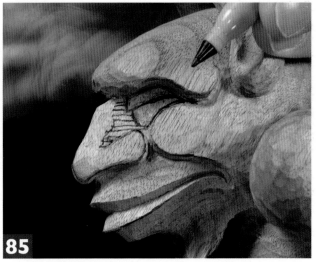

85

Draw in the eyelid and eyeball, as shown. We will be removing waste from around the eye, as indicated by the hash marks.

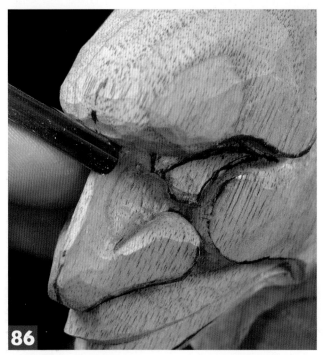

86

Using the ⅛" (3mm) veiner, hollow out this area. Do the other side.

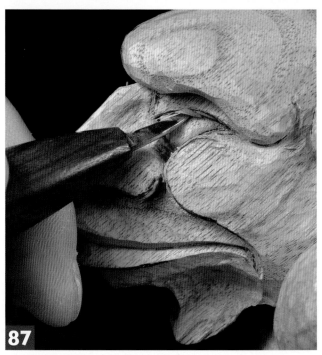

87

Using the detail knife, work on the eyelid and eyeball. Do the other side.

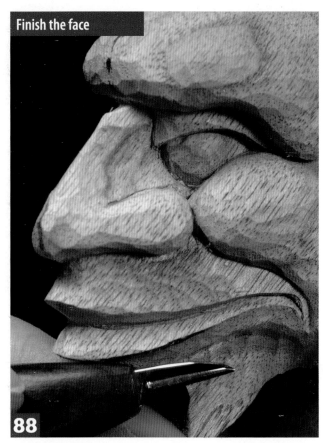

Finish the face

88

Using the detail knife, complete the eye. Also round and shape the brow, nose, and cheek. Do the other side.

89

Examine this view from below and be sure to match up each side. Have them blend at the front. Using your knife, clean up and round off any rough areas. The face is almost complete.

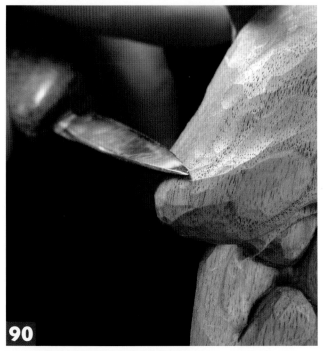

90

Using the knife, give the upper-brow shape by slightly scalloping inward.

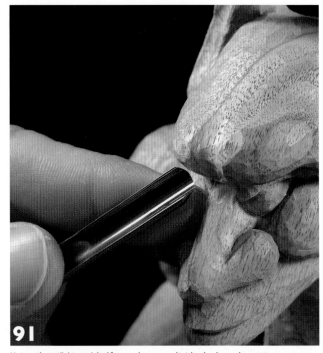

91

Using the ¼" (6mm) half-round gouge, divide the bony brow dead center.

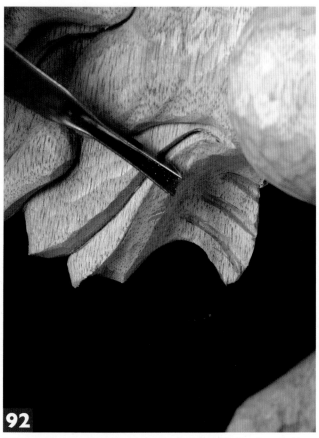

92

A final detail: using the ⅛" (3mm) V-tool, carve three hair lines in each side of the beard.

93

The grotesque is complete and ready for finishing.

Finishing

The finishing process I developed is a bit unconventional, but I took advantage of the natural color of the butternut wood. Be aware this method will not work for basswood. If you will be using basswood, I would suggest using the method from the first project, or another finishing technique of your choice. What makes this method unique for butternut (or a similar tone of wood) is that the natural warm medium-brown color becomes the middle tone of the final desired effect. The tan/beige paint is the highlight, and the brown gel stain is the deepest tone. Another interesting effect from this finishing process is that the overall process accents the open-grained nature of the butternut by making the tiny individual pores stand out, which in turn helps the already present grained appearance more profound. This technique will complement any open-grained wood, such as mahogany and catalpa.

Tools and Materials List

- ■ Disposable stain brush
- ■ 50/50 mix of boiled linseed oil and mineral spirits
- ■ ¼" (6mm) flat brush
- ■ ½" (12mm) flat brush
- ■ Beige or tan acrylic paint
- ■ Rub-on satin polyurethane or regular polyurethane thinned with mineral spirits
- ■ Brown oil-based gel stain (thinned a bit with mineral spirits, if necessary)
- ■ Clean cotton rag
- ■ Latex gloves

1 Using a disposable stain brush, liberally coat the entire carving with a 50/50 mix of boiled linseed oil and mineral spirits. Let it soak in for a few hours.

2 Using a beige or tan acrylic paint and a ½" (12mm) flat brush [¼" (6mm) flat brush for tighter areas], start to highlight the raised areas of the carving. Blend with water, and keep it translucent. This is an interpretive and freehand technique, so take your time and study the photos of the finished piece. Here, I am working on the upper back and arm area.

Next, highlight the face, forearms, and chest.

Apply a light coat with the beige or tan blend to the base.

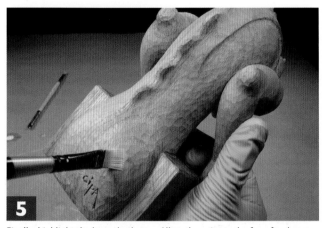

Finally, highlight the lower back area. Allow the paint to dry for a few hours.

Using the disposable stain brush, apply a thin but thorough coat of mineral spirit—thinned satin or regular polyurethane over the entire carving. Apply one coat only. The tan highlighted areas become more translucent as you apply the polyurethane. Let the carving dry overnight.

Apply a brown oil-based gel stain to the entire carving by slathering it on liberally with the stain brush. Thin the stain a bit with mineral spirits if a better flow is needed. Be sure to work it well into the deepest crevices.

The final step is to immediately wipe off the excess gel stain with a clean cotton rag. The deepest unpainted areas will be most affected by the stain. Let the carving dry for a few hours before handling.

The *Screaming* Keystone
Grotesque

For this project, I have chosen to carve a horned pagan visage locked in a terrified scream. The open screaming mouth was actually common, and sometimes was used to serve as a water-spouting gargoyle. I chose a block of butternut for this particular carving because of the warm brown color and moderate grain figure. The keystone would look great hung above an archway or adorning a wall in your home.

Side

Front

Lore

The Romans perfected many architectural feats of engineering. Not least among these is the keystone—a wedge-shaped element that crowns the apex of an archway and locks all other pieces in place. It provides strength to the arch throughout, and allows stresses which otherwise would not be possible. The keystone was the last piece of the arch put into place, and was driven in with blows of a mallet. It is not surprising that the important keystone would be given special decorative attention. Countless medieval keystones sport green men, pagan horned gods, and religious figures.

The horned-god myth is extremely old, far preceding Christianity, Roman, and even Greek belief systems. Cave paintings of a half-man, half-stag figure have been found dating from about 13,000 BC. "Horned God" is a term used to refer to entities

Angled view to show relief.

Close-up of face.

of many cultures and religions: Herne the Hunter, ghost of Windsor Forest in Britain; Pan, Greek god of the woodlands; and even Osiris, Egyptian god of the Underworld. The strongest association is with Cernunnos, the Celtic god of fertility. He was a triumphant hunter, provider, and impregnator of the fertile Mother Goddess.

Cernunnos' stature grew over the ages, and he became known as the guardian to the portal of the Otherworld, and was associated with wealth and prosperity. The horned god became a prime target for the Christian church, which associated him with the devil and the underworld of hell. It is Cernunnos' image that is believed to have been adopted by the church as the image of Satan himself, horns and all—though the pitchfork came much later!

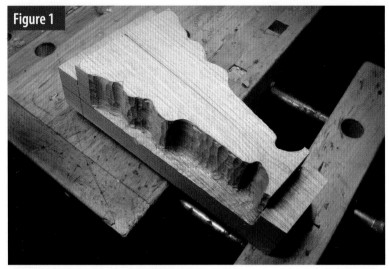

Figure 1

Waste has been removed around the face.

Figure 2

Coat with linseed oil and mineral spirits blend.

Figure 3

Shade the inset areas with black paint.

Artist approach

The block's measurements were 10" x 5" x 3" (25.4cm x 12.7cm x 7.6cm). The nose protrudes furthest at a depth of 3" (7.6cm).

Figure 1 shows the blank after the waste was removed around the face. I left about 1" (2.5cm) of background, leaving a 2" (5cm) depth of material to develop the face. Study the front and side patterns closely. I used a combination of tools, including fishtails, half-round gouges, V-tools, and the trusty knife. I used a rotary grinder with a round burr bit to inset the round pupils. After the face is complete, gently slope the background area with the half-round gouge and the fishtail. Add stylized wavy lines with your V-tool.

To finish the piece, coat the carving with a 50/50 mix of boiled linseed oil and mineral spirits (**Figure 2**). Wait a few hours and wipe the excess off. Next, using a black acrylic paint wash, begin to shade the inset areas (**Figure 3**). This pulls out detail and enhances the carving's three-dimensional quality. Take your time and add as much or as little as you like—just be sure to always add water and smooth out any hard blotchy areas of paint before they set. A rule of thumb is to darken the deeper areas, while leaving the higher or more prominent areas untouched. Blend well between the two differences. Let the carving dry overnight.

Finally, apply three thin coats of satin polyurethane, sanding between each coat with 000 steel wool. After the final coat has dried, buff the entire piece well with 0000 steel wool in order to dull out any glossy areas.

4¾"
(12cm)

3"
(7.6cm)

10"
(25.4cm)

Front

Side

Measurements given show correctly
enlarged size of patterns.

Enlarge Pattern 125%

The Guardian
Grotesque

The image of the ever-vigilant guardian has taken many forms—a lion, a dragon, a fierce dog, a horse, and the Sphinx to name a few. Some are less easily defined, having been created with a more fantastical look. Such is our guardian—he seems to be a combination of several animalistic elements. Nevertheless, he stands at attention, ready to defend against whatever may cross his gaze. Our guardian sculpture is representative of a medieval polymorphic creature. With stylized wings, a serpent's tail, pointy ears, and a lolling tongue, he is very dragon-like with a touch of lion in him. The large-balled toes, stylized neck decoration, and scrolling S-shaped wings are Romanesque in design. Romanesque was an architectural style in Europe during the early 1100s.

Side

Front

Back

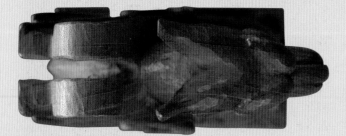

Top

Lore

Guardian sculptures often were placed at the entrances of places of importance, such as temples or governmental establishments. Even today, we still see these proud creatures adorning the steps to banks, libraries, and colleges. The original purpose of the guardian statue depended on what it was defending. Countless holy temples of Far East cultures relied on their guardians to turn away evil and impurity that would attempt to defile the sacred atmosphere. Many Western European cathedrals and churches displayed pairs of lions or gryphons at the main entrance. Some guardians were symbolic of courage, honor, and strength.

Heraldry became a highly developed discipline by the late Middle Ages, with exacting art techniques and strict rules. A person's heraldic coat of arms was used to define a distinction between houses of royalty, rank, and position in society. The symbolic images, or blazons, on the coat of arms would often depict creatures of distinction, such as the rampant lion, horse, dragon, or griffin. No doubt, the images inspired the creation of guardian statues, which appear heraldic in their own right.

Close-up of wings.

Close-up of tail.

Figure 1

Note the difference between the uncarved and carved sides.

Figure 2

Remove waste between the toes with a small half-round gouge.

Artist approach

I have chosen mahogany for this project; it seems an appropriate choice because of the rich, warm color. It is also the wood choice of royal decor. The block size I used is an impressive 12" x 6" x 3" (30.5cm x 15.3cm x 7.6cm). I would encourage you to carve an even larger one after the first go-around. Imagine how impressive it would look on a large scale, placed on your hearth or entranceway!

I used a variety of carving tools for this project, from small to large. Some included half-round gouges, fishtails, V-tools, veiners, skew chisels, and knives. Some power tools such as a drill press and a rotary grinder were of use as well.

The blank should be band sawed out from the side view. Because the stock is only 3" (7.6cm) thick, it is not necessary to try to saw from the front view. I have included patterns for the front and back views for reference only. The void area underneath between the belly, legs, and tail can be hogged out by use of a large drill bit (such as a spade), and then cleaned up with hand tools. Because the long curving tongue is a bit fragile, it would be best to wait until the carving has progressed a good deal before removing the void between it and the chest.

Figure 1 shows basic blocking out without rounding any specific areas. Notice the hash marks of the front profile as of yet uncarved on one side. The wings are the outermost projections on the sides, so these must be defined first.

Figure 2 shows the attention paid to the toes. I am using a small half-round gouge here to remove waste between the toes. Later, the toes can be fully shaped with a knife.

The wings, legs, and tail are now fully formed.

The waste between the wings must be removed by hand.

Create the void in the mouth with a rotary tool.

In **Figure 3**, we can see considerable progress on the body. The wings are fully formed, as well as the legs and tail. Notice the void area between the tongue and chest has been finally removed.

Figure 4 shows a rear view. The void to be removed between the wings is rather deep, and must be done by hand. Using a saw (unless it is a very small one), risks damaging the back of the neck and head. Use small half-round gouges to remove the waste, and then fishtails to smooth out and clean up the inner surfaces.

Figure 5 shows progress on the head. I am using the rotary tool to help create the small void inside the mouth. This can certainly be done by hand with small detail tools, but with more difficulty.

I finished the carving with several coats of thinned polyurethane, sanding gently between coats with 000 steel wool. Finally, I buffed it to a dull sheen with 0000 steel wool.

6"
(15.2cm)

12"
(30.5cm)

CIPA

Side

Measurements given
show correctly enlarged
size of patterns.

**Enlarge Pattern
135%**

3"
(7.6cm)

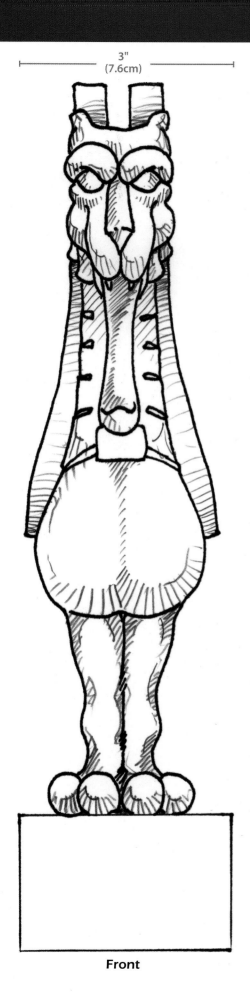

Front

**Enlarge Pattern
135%**

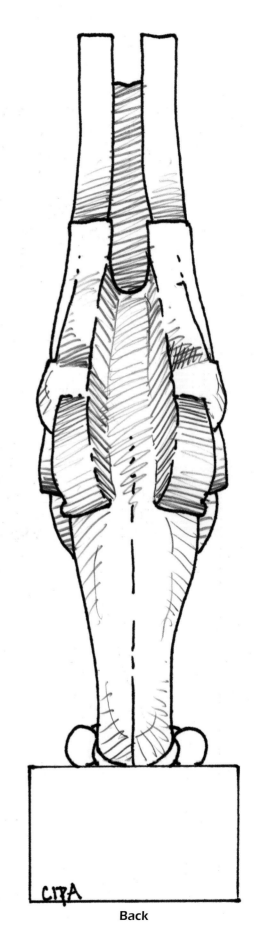

Back

The Green Man
Door Knocker

I have chosen to depict our Green Man as a door knocker—an item that is both functional and aesthetic. In reality, a functional door knocker would have been made of brass or iron; wood would have never stood up to the elements and abuse it would have had to endure. Regardless, I have created a design that provides for a moving knocker to be banged against a strike plate. I daresay this carving would also fall short of endurance if you would choose to display it on your door as a working model, but certainly it could be displayed on the wall, or perhaps on the inside of a door for decorative purposes. I'm sure there are things we could modify in order to make it more durable and functional, but I will leave that to your imagination and ingenuity.

Side

Front ¾ view

Lore

Images of the Green Man, or Jack O' the Green, are as varied and diverse as nature itself. There is no single definition of form possible, because he encompasses a multitude of variations on the theme. However, one characteristic remains true to all Green Men: their facial features are always entwined with leafy foliage, sometimes sprouting from their mouths, nostrils, and eyes. Some retain more humanistic features with just a hint of leaf, as if it were an afterthought, where others sport so much foliage we can barely discern any facial features at all. What has become the Green Man is rooted from the collective creations of thousands of stonemasons and woodcarvers from the medieval age to present.

The Green Man comes to us from pagan tradition. He represented the spirits of the trees, plants, and all foliage. He had control over nature, could make it rain, and was primarily responsible for successful crops planted by ancient Celtic people. As a promoter of growth, he represented fertility as well as regeneration. He is a primitive reminder to us that we live on a planet that is still, despite all humankind's attempts, ultimately ruled by nature.

The Green Man has been cleverly integrated into classic architecture throughout the ages. Known as one of the oldest forms of grotesque modeling, he can be found inside and outside churches and cathedrals all over Western Europe. It is odd that the Christian church so readily adopted such an established symbol of paganism. Nevertheless, the Green Man is found there quite liberally, intertwined amongst the saints and other iconography.

Close-up of face.

Close-up of door knocker assembly.

Artist approach

I used catalpa as the wood species for this particular piece. The natural grayish-brown color easily adapts to a green tint, and it has a very profound grain, which helps to accent the contour variations in our Green Man. There are three main parts to the doorknocker:

- Face/striker plate, block measuring 10" x 6" (25.4cm x 15.2cm), 2" (5cm) thick
- Knocker, two blocks each measuring 5" x 5" (12.7cm x 12.7cm) square, 1½" (3.8cm) thick
- Lower jaw piece, block measuring 2¼" x 1½" (5.7cm x 3.8cm), 1" (2.5cm) thick

I used a minimum of carving tools for this project—a few shallow gouges, a small half-round gouge, a fishtail, a V-tool, and a knife.

Even as a decorative piece, there must be some strength to the knocker, otherwise the horizontal bar (mouthpiece) will surely crack because of the short grain in that area. If you try to face the grain the other way, it will most likely snap one of the vertical arms. The solution here is to laminate (glue) two pieces together: the top piece with vertically running grain, and the lower piece with horizontally running grain (see **Figure 1**). With a sander, planer, or joiner, be sure the two sides to be glued are perfectly flush and flat so you have a nice seamless glue joint. Clamp them tightly together while the glue dries. The inner-waste portion of the knocker can be largely removed with a drill and a large drill bit. The rest will need to be done by hand.

The underside of the ball portion needs to be flattened so it rests against the striker plate when assembled. When carving the arm and mouthpiece areas, be sure the glue joint is evenly split between the top and bottom to ensure an equal strength of both grain directions.

After all parts are carved, they need to be assembled. The upper horizontal bar will need to fit loosely up into the cavity carved out underneath the upper lip of the Green Man. Once the bar is in place, the lower jaw should be glued onto the striker plate and positioned in a manner that locks in the knocker, but not so tightly that it cannot move freely. This procedure will take a few dry runs and some tweaking with your knife before you are satisfied with the fit. If this is done well, the finished product should appear seamless, as if it were carved of one whole piece. Refer to **Figure 2** for a better look at this area.

For finishing, I have essentially used the same technique as with the Screaming Keystone Grotesque (please refer to pages 86 to 91), with a few minor changes. Before applying the 50/50 linseed oil and mineral spirit mixture, I tinted it with a bit of green oil paint. For the acrylic paint, I used a forest green color.

Figure 1

Use two pieces of wood to create the knocker.

Figure 2

The knocker bar, lower jaw and upper lip need to be carefully placed.

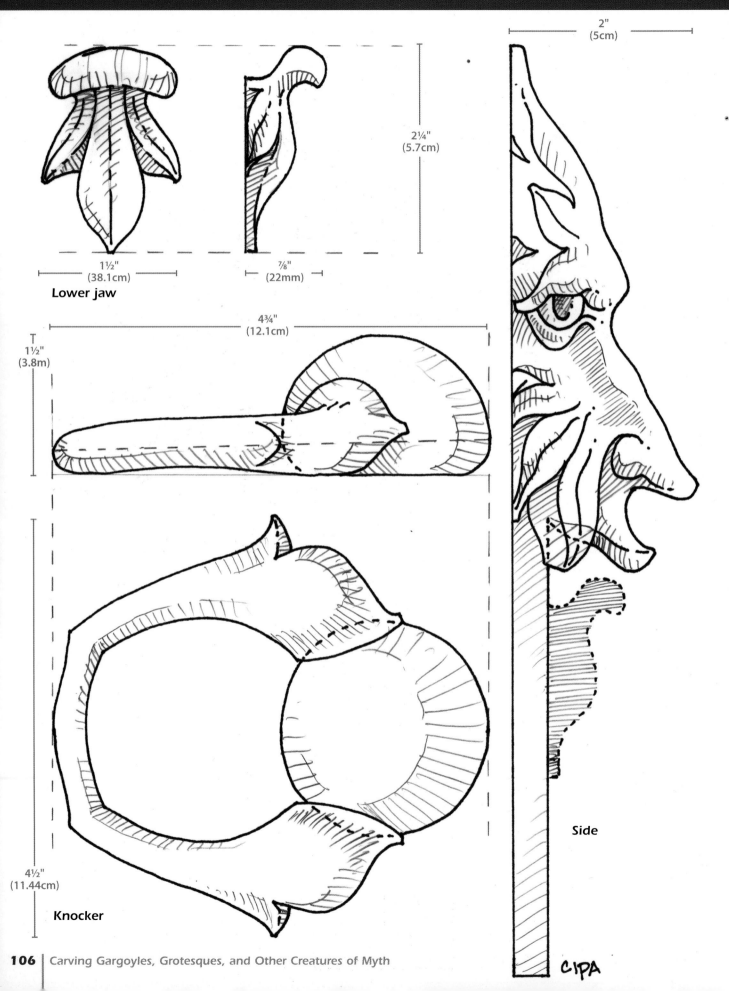

2¼"
(5.7cm)

1½"
(38.1cm)

⅞"
(22mm)

Lower jaw

4¾"
(12.1cm)

1½"
(3.8m)

2"
(5cm)

4½"
(11.44cm)

Knocker

Side

CIPA

6"
(15.2cm)

9¾"
(24.8cm)

Front

The Corbel
with Grotesque

Our corbel project is of a fantastical design; there is some scrollwork, a grotesque monkey like head, and some wing stylization going on. The swirls and recesses require special care when carving. Though you probably won't use the corbel in a traditional capacity—to support a roof or a real gargoyle—this piece could be hung on your wall and used to support a small trinket or candle, or several of them could be used to support a shelf.

Side

Front

Lore

A corbel is a load-bearing bracket common in medieval architecture. It is still used today. The word comes from the Old French for raven or crow, due to the corbel's often beak-like appearance.

The brackets supported jutting structures. For vaults, a number of smaller corbels were set deeply into the wall's surface. For balconies, the corbels were large and elaborately designed. Lone corbels supported a lamp or even a gargoyle or grotesque. Inside a building, richly carved corbels supported windowsills or mantelpieces.

Regardless of use, corbels were usually highly decorated. Many had Romanesque-style scrollwork; others had acanthus leaves and other forms of foliage. Many had grotesques, animal or human heads, fantastic creatures, and religious subjects as part of their design.

Artist approach

The block of jelutong is $9^1/2$" x 6" x $2^3/4$" (24.1cm x 15.2cm x 7cm). The top shelf piece is $6^1/4$" x 3" x $3/8$" (15.9cm x 7.6cm x 10mm). I chose yellowwood because it resembled the finished corbel's color.

Band saw the block using the side-view pattern; the front view is for reference only. **Figure 1** shows the beginning stage of the blank, with only the upper scroll (the outermost feature) defined.

Figure 2 shows all of the elements blocked out. At this point, the details begin. Both sides are identical, so you need only to join them together on the front. When carving the shelf support, keep it as uniform and square as possible, as if you have used a router with a round-over bit.

I finished the corbel with tung oil. Normally no more than four coats of

Figure 1

The rough out with carved scroll.

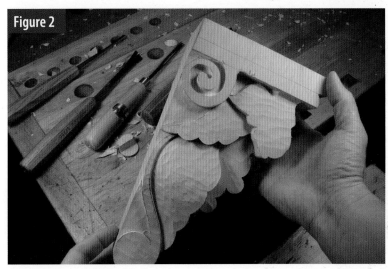

Figure 2

The elements are blocked out.

tung oil should be applied, but jelutong is particularly absorbent and needs six coats. I lightly buffed the carving with 0000 steel wool in between the last few coats. Once cured, I treated the piece with a healthy dose of an orange (antique pine or cedar) gel stain. Once applied, I waited a few minutes and wiped off the excess. Once dry, I glued on the separately finished shelf piece, using clamps to hold it in place while drying. Finally, an inset keyhole-style hanger was installed in the back for hanging purposes.

Close-up of curved lines.

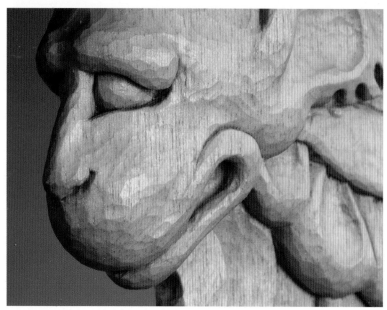

Close-up of face.

2³⁄₈"
(6cm)

Front

5⅞"
(15cm)

9½"
(24.1cm)

Side

CiPA

The Crouching
Imp

This unhappy looking fellow is representative of what most people probably think of when they hear the word gargoyle—a bat-winged, crouching, and devilish figure waiting to pounce on an unsuspecting passerby. As we now know, this is a classic example of a grotesque, being non-functional and purely ornamental. As mentioned before, he has a decidedly unhappy expression, probably because he has been forced to perch upon a cathedral rooftop, entombed in stone, to forever guard the entranceway. Or, maybe he is sad because he has no thumbs...

Side

Back

Front

Top

Lore

This fellow is actually an imp, and he does have a history. The imp mythology most likely has Germanic origins, although it spread to many parts of Western Europe by the 1500s. The imp has most been described as something of a cross between a devil and a fairy; small in stature, they were considered very mischievous and lively. They were lesser beings in the demonic world, and were not as dangerous as other supernatural beings.

Imps were often associated with witches and magicians. More commonly referred to as a witch's familiar, imps were trapped into an existence of servitude by the commanding witch. It was said one could capture and trap an imp in a bottle or small vial by using certain incantations that appealed to the Holy Trinity, as described in the French eighteenth-century grimoire (book of spells) *Le Secret des Secrets*. Once trapped, the imp could be commanded to carry out evil tasks against innocent people.

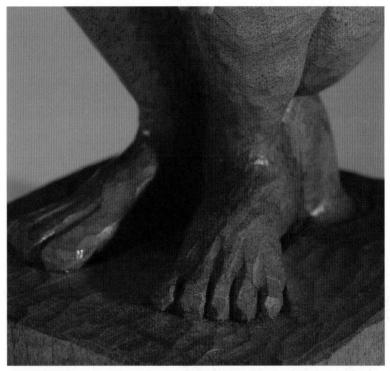

Close-up of feet.

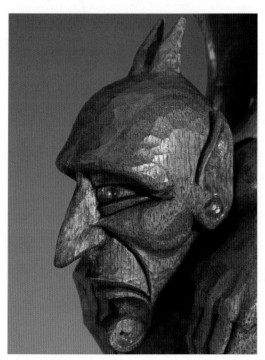

Close-up of face.

As a reward, the witch supposedly allowed the imp to suckle blood from their fingertips or blemishes, such as warts.

Probably the most famous historical account of impish servitude was by a fifteenth-century Swiss alchemist named Paracelsus. Paracelsus was a most outspoken man of his time. Known mainly for his unconventional medical practices, he combined natural healing with magic and Christian beliefs. Paracelsus actually has been attributed to identifying many healing herbs used today, and was one of the first to recognize the body will heal itself of a wound if infection is first removed. In any case, Paracelsus believed spirits of nature could be used for healing, and benevolent imps were sought after. It is said the alchemist had an imp by the name of Zoyh trapped forever in the crystal pommel of his sword. The sword of Paracelsus is actually quite famous, and quite lost. Many have searched for it, and many search still.

Figure 1

The basic shapes have been blocked out.

Artist approach

I have carved our imp out of a solid block of mahogany measuring 8" x 3¼" x 4¾" (20.3cm x 8.3cm x 12.1cm). The grain runs vertically, and the base is about 1" (2.5cm) thick. This piece turned out to be one of the more difficult carvings to complete in this book, as the position of the imp is unusual and physically impossible (go ahead, try it). The larger you go with this project, the easier it will be to accomplish, as well as being more impressive.

His body is humanoid, with an overly large head, elongated hands, and bat-like wings. He sits upon a small lump provided for strength, and the detail between his legs is non-existent. As an actual stone-carved piece, this absence of detail would have been likely, since it would not be seen from a distance anyway.

I have provided a few progress images. In **Figure 1,** you can clearly see I have blocked out the basic shapes. The shoulder sections, which are the outermost prominent side features, stand apart from the head and body. It is always best to keep things squared off until you know you have each side equally proportioned. Once this is done, you can start to shape and round the various elements, as shown in **Figure 2**. Be sure to splay the feet apart, as opposed to carving them tightly together.

One helpful tip is to use a pull saw to remove the waste material between the wings, as shown in **Figure 3**. Make sure this is one of your last roughing-in details; the grain configuration combined with the small connector to the body could become fragile and may crack when applying stress while carving other areas.

I used a variety of tools on this project: practically my whole arsenal. The final details, as always, were mostly done with a knife. I did use a rotary tool to help remove waste in the tight area between the hands and cheeks.

The imp was finished simply with a few coats of satin polyurethane, sanding between each coat with 000 steel wool, and buffing afterward with 0000 steel wool in order to dull out any glossy areas.

Figure 2

The elements have been shaped.

Figure 3

The waste between the wings can be removed with a pull saw.

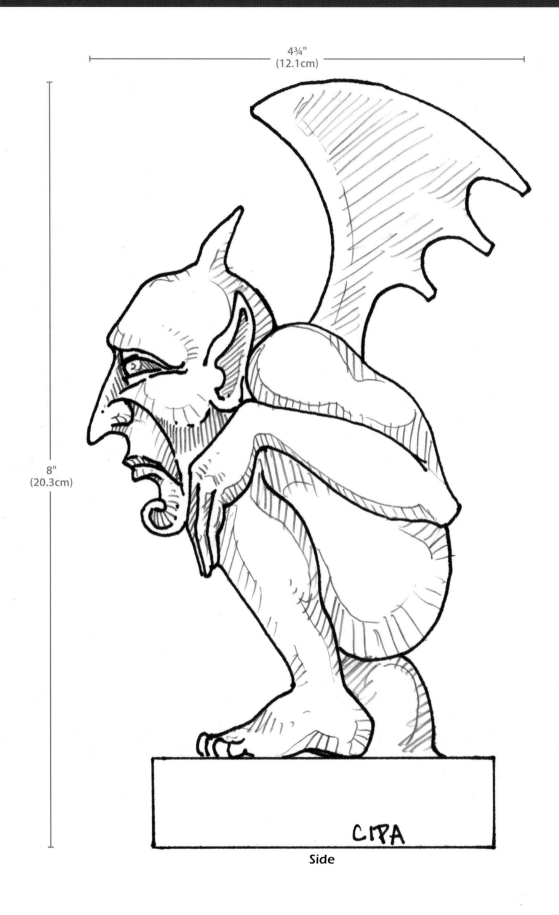

4¾"
(12.1cm)

8"
(20.3cm)

CIPA

Side

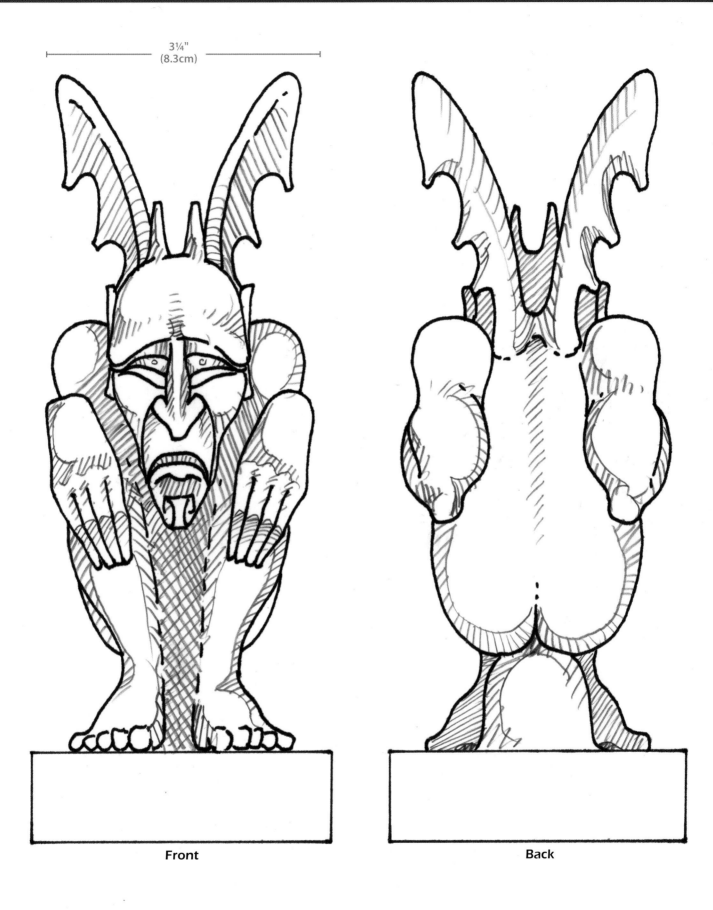

3¼"
(8.3cm)

Front

Back

The Intaglio Lion
Medallion

I have designed this project to represent the lion in a more medieval stylized quality; he is certainly not anatomically correct, but is unmistakably leonine in nature. He sports a stylized scale-like mane, a long tail, and a toothy grimace.

I have also chosen to represent the carving in an intaglio style. Intaglio in Italian literally means carving, but more precisely refers to incising. Intaglio in the two-dimensional sense is a printmaking technique, but when it refers to stone carving, it becomes a type of relief work. You could call our project piece bas-relief, which means the background is cut away to reveal the subject, but technically our subject is below the surface of the overall block, thus being incised. This carving technique was used extensively on cathedrals and basilicas found in Italy, such as the building of San Leonardo of Siponto. Although the ancient town of Siponto was abandoned after earthquakes in the thirteenth century, this structure still stands and boasts much sophisticated intaglio stonework.

Close-up of gap between tail and plaque.

Close-up of face and tail tuft.

Neck detail.

Body and foot detail.

Lore

The lion is used repeatedly and above all other creatures in medieval artistry. From coat of arms heraldry to gargoyles, the King of the Beasts has symbolized courage, royalty, and Christian iconography. The lion was shown by these artists to be the first animal on and off Noah's ark.

The subject matter of many gargoyles and grotesques found on Western European churches and cathedrals appeared to be of a species that is unclear; many were composites of several creatures, and others seemed to be of their own ilk altogether. However, many seemed quite leonine in nature, despite some strange anatomical variations. The typical artist of the Middle Ages had little opportunity to witness a lion firsthand, so they often used creative license. The central theme when carving a leonine creature was always the mane; however, sometimes the artist included hoofed feet, wings, and long, snake-like tongues.

The lion was ultimately a symbol of Christ, the Lion of the tribe of Judah. According to the medieval bestiaries and Christian allegory, the three main "natures" of the lion each had a meaning. Supposedly, the lion would erase its tracks with its tail, which was linked with Christ's ability to escape the devil and conceal his divine identity. It was also said that the lion always slept with its eyes open, representing Jesus—physically dead after crucifixion, but still spiritually alive in his divine nature. Lastly, it was believed that the lioness always gave birth to dead cubs, and the father lion roared over them to bring them to life. This was meant to represent how God woke Jesus after three days in his tomb.

The other natures of the lion are taken as examples of how people are to live morally. The church said that just as the lion will not attack a fallen man or anger unless injured, and will allow captive men to depart, people should be slow to anger and quick to forgive. Finally, gargoyle lions would often be shown stamping upon a small dragon creature. The dragon symbolized sin, and Christ's triumph over it.

Close-up of head and tail gap.

Angled view to show relief.

Artist approach

I used basswood for this project. The panel started at 1¼" (3.2cm) thick and measured 8½" (21.6cm) square. Although basswood panels of this size are not hard to find, I laminated two pieces together in order to achieve this size. Tools used for this project included spoon gouges, fishtails, a skew chisel, assorted detail tools, and a knife. **Figure 1** shows the background removed, which is where the spoon gouges come in

handy. **Figure 2** shows partial figuring of the subject.

Once the lion is carved, the background must be leveled and then textured with a stamping tool. A stamping tool is a punch with a flat cutting tip with teeth or a pattern embossed on the surface. When you tap the punch onto the surface with your mallet, it leaves an impression. The impression must be applied many times and overlapped, so the overall effect is that of a stippled surface. This helps to pull the subject matter out from the background by diffusing the light reflected from it. Stamping tools are a common requirement for relief carvers and can be easily acquired from a woodcarving supplier.

To finish the piece, I first coated the carving with a 50/50 mix of boiled linseed oil and mineral spirits. After the carving dried overnight, I applied three coats of thinned polyurethane, sanding a bit with 000 steel wool between coats. Once the polyurethane was dry, I gave it a final buff with 0000 steel wool. I then slathered the piece with an orange-brown gel stain, such as cedar or antique pine, and immediately wiped off any excess. The stain helps to deepen the detail; I used the orange-brown color so it would be subtle, as opposed to using a darker brown stain.

Figure 1

The background has been removed.

Figure 2

The lion has been partially shaped.

7⅝"
(19.4cm)

7⅝"
(19.4cm)

Outside block 8½"
(21.6cm)

The Demon
Gargoyle

This project is provided as a secondary example of a traditional water-spouting gargoyle, one that could easily be found atop a French cathedral. The variance here is this one would have been built into the pitch of a sloping rooftop, hanging out over the vaulted edge. As a functional gutter, this design would have been most effective, throwing the water well beyond the edge of the wall below. I have carved in the actual water trough and hole into the mouth where water would have dispersed as a working model. Again, the feature is purely optional.

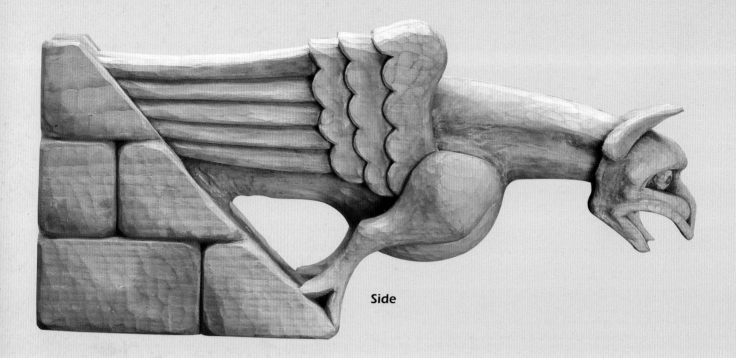

Side

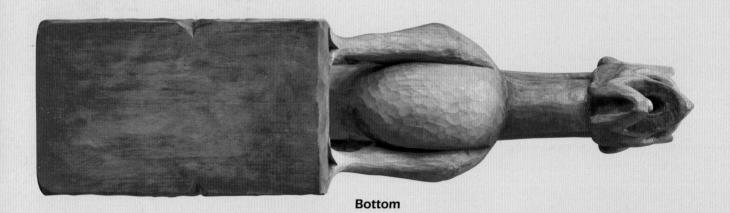

Bottom

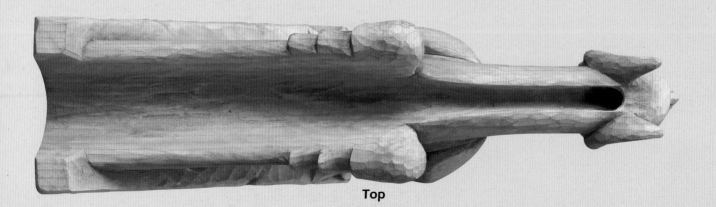

Top

Lore

Many gargoyles found atop churches and cathedrals were undoubtedly intended to intimidate and frighten attendees and passersby. No one was alone with these grisly, ever-watching stone sentinels, and no activity escaped their notice. Why else were so many ugly and frightening creatures, easily interpreted as demons, placed on church tops, as if they had landed there to leer at those below?

From a biblical, or at least a medieval perspective, demons inhabit the middle air, caught between the heaven above and the earth below. That concept could partially explain why the gargoyles were perched above, and were so numerous.

The fact that such ugliness was permitted to reside among the countless images of beautiful religious art presents a symbolic metaphor of the notion that the devil is helping God by carrying out the punishment of the sinful. The devil and his minions, as God's adversaries, have their rightful place in the grand design of converting sinners into faith, and condemning those who do not.

Face detail.

Wall, wing, and feet detail.

Front

Artist approach

I carved the piece from a basswood block measuring 11" x 5" x 3" (27.9cm x 12.7cm x 7.6cm). The carving tasks are straightforward, and should not provide too much difficulty. A hand drill or drill press should be used to hog out waste in the area between the outstretched legs, the belly, and the slanted base. From the front view, the area between the legs should be done by hand using carving tools.

The finishing technique employed is identical to the one used for the first step-by-step project in this book. Please refer to pages 55 to 57, or feel free to apply one of the other techniques described throughout the book. A keyhole hanger will need to be installed on the back so that the project may be hung on a wall or other vertical surface; however, this carving will stand up on its own as well.

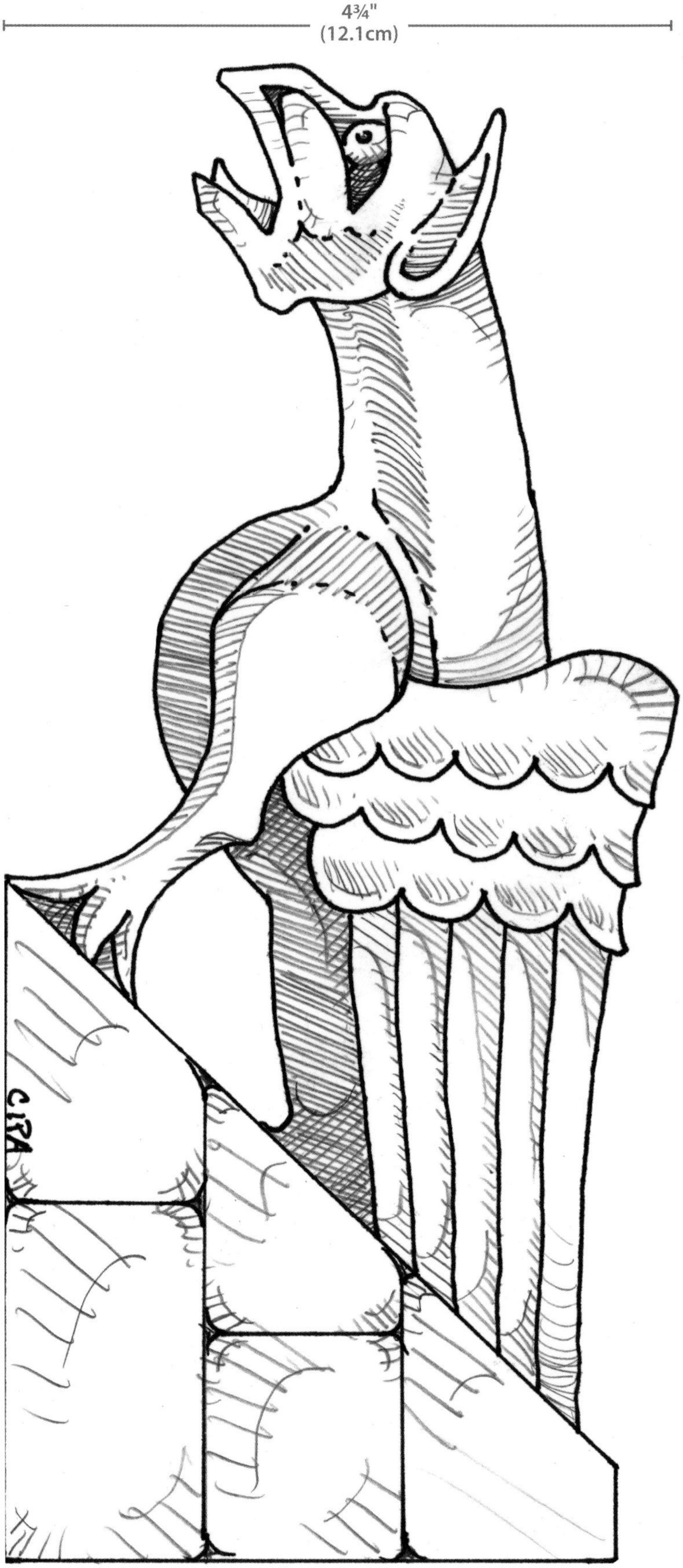

4¾"
(12.1cm)

Measurements given show correctly enlarged size of patterns.

Side

Enlarge Pattern 120%

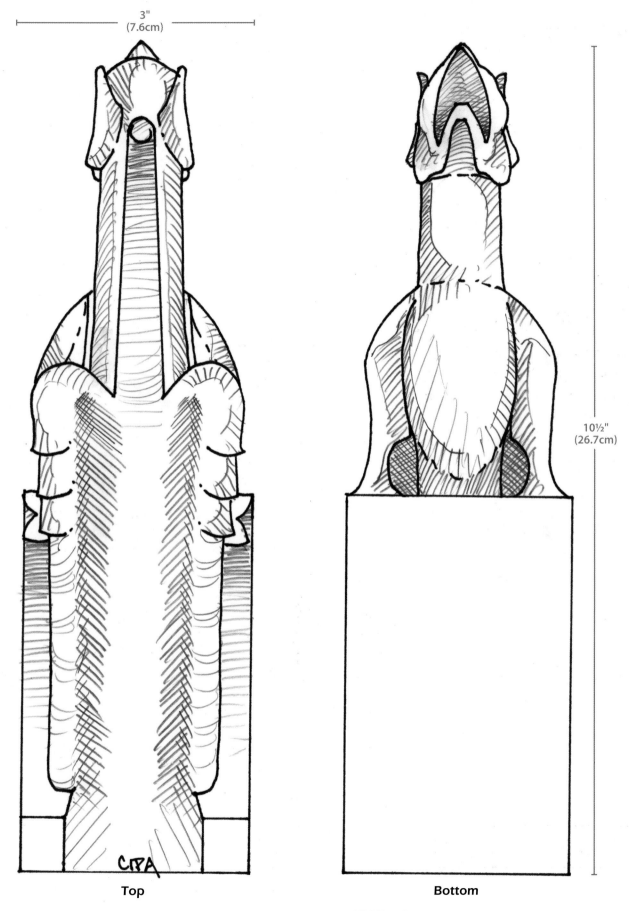

3"
(7.6cm)

10½"
(26.7cm)

Top

Bottom

Enlarge Pattern 120%

The Gargoyle
Cane

When I first thought about writing a book on carving gargoyles, I admittedly knew next to nothing about them. I have done exhaustive research in order to know my subject better. Once I was more educated about this mysterious art form, I wondered how I could integrate it with a subject dearer to my heart, and here it is. I love, above all else, to carve canes and walking sticks. One thought that crossed my mind when I first studied images of classic waterspout, or "true" gargoyles, was: "Man, that would make a great cane handle!" The waterspout gargoyle's shape is indeed a perfect shape for such a project; the only thing to figure out was how to work the design into a shaft, and how to make it strong enough to support weight. The design I have presented here is typical of a classic Notre Dame cathedral gargoyle. I have arched the overall shape a bit in order to have it fit the hand better, and I omitted the drainage channel that normally would run the length of the carving.

Full cane and handle

Front

Back

Top

Bottom

Artist approach

I used mahogany for the handle. Mahogany is strong, but not too hard to carve. Avoid using a softer wood such as basswood for this project, as it may easily snap when in use. Even better would be a much harder wood such as cherry or maple, but they can be quite difficult to carve. However, with sharp tools and a lot of patience, it can certainly be accomplished if you wish to go this route. The shaft is swamp maple. I chose swamp maple because I like the bark. You can choose just about anything you would like for the shaft, but be sure it is strong and resistant to dents. It is important that the total diameter where the shaft joins the handle is no more than 1¹/₂" (3.8cm), otherwise you will not be able to taper the sleeve to a seamless fit—1¹/₄" (3.2cm) would be preferable. Cut the shaft's overall length longer than you think you will need—you will be able to cut it down when it is all together later.

Close-up of head.

The first thing to do is to prepare the block for carving. Because of stress issues when the cane is under normal use, make sure the grain runs both ways—along the handle and along the shaft sleeve. This would be impossible to accomplish with a single piece of wood, so glue two together. You can see the different grain directions are indicated in **Figure 1**. This step should be done before band sawing out the shape, so you can adequately clamp the two together. The handle block should measure 7½" x 2½" (19.1cm x 6.4cm), and should be about 1½" (3.8cm) thick. The shaft sleeve block should measure at least 2¾" (7cm) long, and 1½" (3.8cm) square. Be sure the adjoining surfaces to be glued together are perfectly flush with each other to ensure a tight, seamless glue joint. Once the two blocks have been joined and the glue is cured, a ¼" (6mm) hole needs to be drilled through the length of the shaft sleeve, and all the way through the handle as well. Find your center before this task, and drill the hole as straight and true as possible (refer to the pattern). You will need a long bit, and a drill press would be best, although not necessary. You may now band saw the shape of the gargoyle into the overall handle blank.

Prepare the shaft by first drilling a ¼" (6mm) hole down through the center; you should go at least 4" (10.2cm) deep. Again, drill the hole as straight and true as possible. You will not be able to maneuver this around a drill press, so you will need to clamp it down and use a hand drill. Next, using a knife, start to shape ¾"- (19mm-) diameter male tenon. Take your time with this and measure often. Be sure the butt joint is perfectly flat so the two elements join nicely.

Two blocks with different grain directions make the handle.

Place steel rod in the drill holes.

On the handle, you will need to create a corresponding female mortise. You could use a spade drill bit for this, but you run the risk of tearing out more than is necessary. I actually did it by hand, using a long-bladed knife. With short turns of the wrist, I slowly bored out a ³/₄" (19mm) hole starting with the pre-drilled hole. Keep trying to fit the two into place until you have removed enough waste to do so. Getting the two

pieces to fit snugly is a delicate operation, and should not be rushed. Remember, you are not building a piece of furniture, so it does not have to be perfectly symmetrical; it only needs to look good and fit tightly. Study the photo closely—you can get a good idea of how it should all look.

Once you have accomplished the fitting, acquire a length of threaded ¹/₄" (6mm) steel rod to place in the drill holes. This will help to strengthen the overall cane (**Figure 2**). Cut the rod so that, when inserted, it will fall short of protruding through the top by about ¹/₂" (12mm). Insert yellow wood glue into the holes and smear it onto the tenon. Then, push the handle and shaft together. Hopefully, the ¹/₄" (6mm) rod will fit tightly so you can twist and actually screw the parts together. This will help to keep them together while the glue dries. Immediately wipe off the glue squeeze-out with a damp cloth.

Carve the mortar lines on the handle and the shaft.

Once the glue has cured, you may begin your carving. Be sure to taper the sleeve with a knife closely to the diameter of the shaft so it is seamless to the touch. After that, you may carve the mortar lines past the mahogany down into the shaft wood (**Figure 3**).

Once the piece is fully carved, the ¹/₄" (6mm) hole on top must be plugged. Carve a small piece of mahogany to plug the hole tightly. Glue it into place, as shown in **Figure 4**. Once dry, you may carve the excess off to create a flush surface.

To finish, I simply applied a few coats of polyurethane, sanding lightly between each coat with 000 steel wool, and buffing out the final coat with 0000 steel wool.

Glue a mahogany plug into the hole.

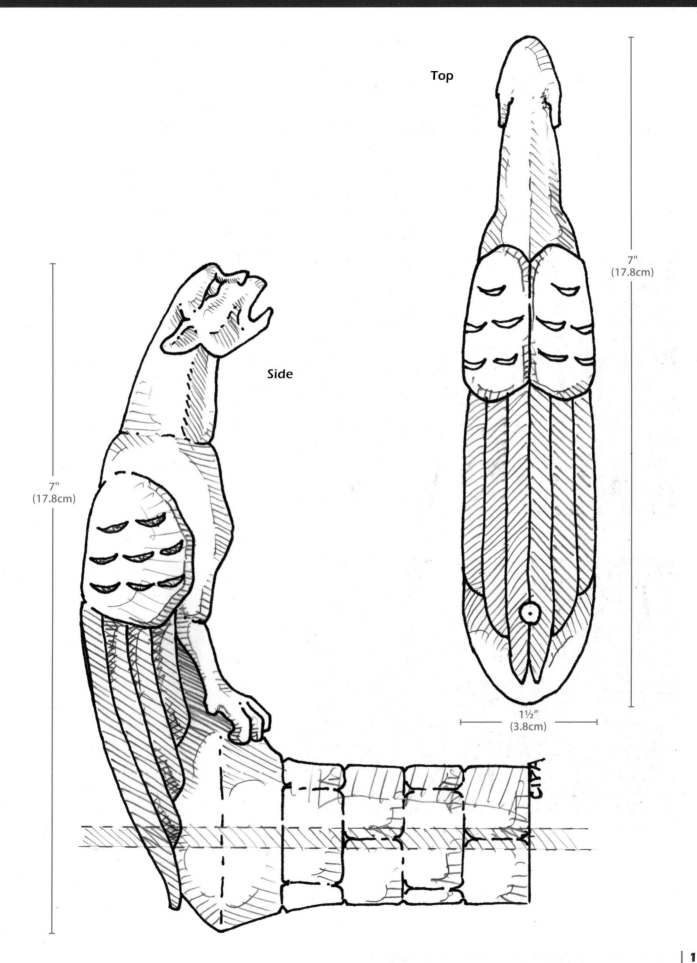

Top

7"
(17.8cm)

Side

7"
(17.8cm)

1½"
(3.8cm)

The Chimera

Our chimera consists of a dragon body (with bird-like qualities), topped with the Romanesque head of a woman. This design was inspired by the Harpies, creatures of Greek mythology. The Harpies were bird-women, monstrous and cruel, with vulture-like bodies and the heads of hags. My version is decidedly less vile, and a bit more regal. This design is an appliqué, which is a deep bas-relief effect. This design would most likely have been carved out of a vertical stone surface as pure ornamentation. I have chosen to display only the subject matter, but you may choose to carve it from a panel, leaving the background. You could also carve it as I have and mount it onto a surface of a contrasting species of wood.

Front

Side

Top

Bottom

Lore

The Chimera was originally a Greek mythological beast from Lycia. The fire-breathing female creature was composed of parts from multiple animals, specifically a lion's body and head, an additional head of a goat, and a serpent or dragon at the tail. The hero Bellerophon, riding the winged horse Pegasus, was finally able to slay the Chimera by wedging a block of lead in her throat, which melted and suffocated her.

Since then and into modern times, the term *chimera* has taken on a catch-all meaning, used to describe any imaginary creature of polymorphic design. The combinations are boundless, and are especially unique when the human factor is added. Artists of the Middle Ages almost exclusively depicted imaginary creatures on a routine basis, as they had very little or no reference material to choose from. Medieval bestiaries were wildly inaccurate, and often were assembled from accounts and stories from travelers abroad.

Gargoyles were a favorite subject for new polymorphic designs, and countless creatures were invented by simply combining known animal parts with human ones. The dragon was depicted most often in its many varieties, and was often combined with the human head, as our project example shows.

Foot detail.

Wing detail.

Face detail.

Wing detail.

Artist approach

I carved the piece from a 2¼" (5.7cm) thick basswood block measuring 7¾" x 7½" (19.7cm x 19cm). The carving techniques are those of deep relief work, and should not provide too much difficulty. A hand drill or drill press should be used to hog out waste in the area between the head and wings; the smaller areas between the tail, feet, and belly should be done by hand, using carving tools. I used a combination of tools, from fishtails and half-round gouges to a V-tool and knife.

The finishing technique employed is identical to the one used for the first step-by-step project in this book, except that instead of grey paint for the lowlights, I decided to use a sage green. This imparted the piece with an overall verdigris effect. Please refer to page 55 for an explanation of this method, or feel free to apply one of the other techniques described throughout.

A keyhole hanger will need to be installed on the back so the project may be hung on a wall or other vertical surface.

7¼"
(18.4cm)

7¼"
(18.4cm)

Front

The Woodcarver

This grotesque is an example of the human variety, which although not as numerous as the anamorphic types, were just as often bizarre in reference to their anatomy. Some were mildly humorous, such as our fellow, while others were downright bawdy. The large eyes, uncomfortable leg posture, and the silly smile all help to give this carving its amusing air. Notice that I have not included much detail on the chest area. As mentioned earlier, this was a common occurrence with gargoyles and grotesques, as the common observer couldn't make out many details from the ground. If you wish, you may add more detail. However, note that these are difficult areas to embellish. Be careful not to break off the hands and tools.

Front

Side

Top

Bottom

Lore

There were many different reasons for depicting humans as gargoyles and grotesques. Satire was chief among these reasons, which provided much-needed humor to the mostly illiterate townsfolk. Face pullers, with water spouting from their mouths, were common, while others were shown performing acts of lewd behavior (use your imagination). Some human gargoyles were used to mock human vices, such as drunkenness, gambling, blaspheming, laziness, gluttony, and greed.

There was a medieval belief that physical ugliness, deformity, and sickness were associated with evil, while physical beauty was symbolic of goodness. This could be a good reason why most human gargoyles were anatomically imperfect. In contrast, this also explains why medieval religious figures, such as Christ and Mary, were shown as beautiful images.

Many human gargoyles and grotesques, especially those erected much later during the Victorian era, were tributes to the working man, and represented specific occupations. Among them were lofty positions, such as the scholar, philosopher, physician, and politician. Others celebrated the blue-collar worker, such as the bricklayer and farmer. Even the stone mason who did the carving of the sculptures sometimes snuck his own visage in for posterity.

I have chosen, as homage to you, the reader and fellow woodcarver, to depict a humble woodcarving fellow with chisel and mallet in hand. The impossible posture shown is very typical of the satirical grotesques, which often were found crammed up into the eve of a ledge, or as a corbel supporting yet another gargoyle of larger proportions.

Artist approach

For this project, I chose a 3" (7.6cm) thick block of basswood measuring 6" x 7¼" (15.2cm x 18.4cm). The outermost parts of the carving are the fisted hands, which are the only remaining areas at a thickness of 3" (7.6cm).

Figure 1 shows the hands and tools section roughed out as the most prominent feature. When removing wood from around the facial area, leave enough for the nose; otherwise you will end up with a very flattened face.

Figure 1

The project has been roughed out.

Figure 2

Waste has been deeply removed around the hands.

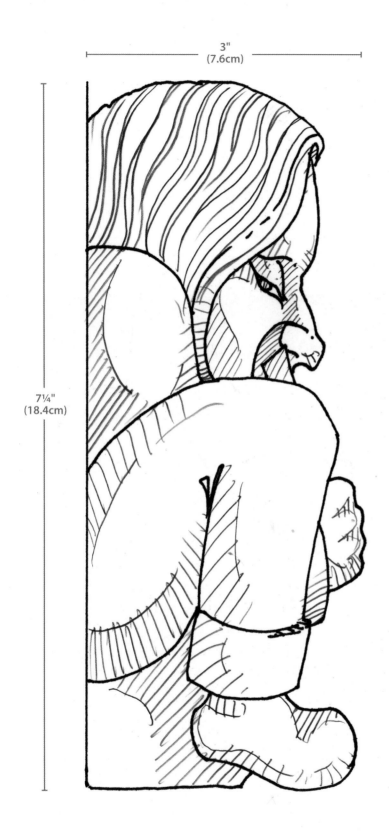

3"
(7.6cm)

7¼"
(18.4cm)

Figure 2 shows progress in the hands and tools area, with waste removed deeply around them. This area will become fragile—be sure to leave waste wood behind the chisel and mallet for support until the very last minute. Once you have completed the details, carefully remove the waste from behind without putting too much pressure in this area. Keep the cyanoacrylate glue handy in case you suffer a crack!

When shaping the whole piece, study the relationship between the front and side patterns. The side view is for reference purposes only. I used a combination of tools, from fishtails and half-round gouges to a V-tool and the trusty knife. I used a Dremel rotary grinder with a round burr bit to help get into the deepest spots.

To finish the piece, I tried something different—a commercial white pickling stain applied heavily with a brush. Wait a few hours and wipe off the excess. Apply a few more coats until you have the desired effect. Let it dry overnight. Next, use a wash mix of raw sienna acrylic paint to shade the inset areas around the carving. This pulls out detail and enhances the carving's three-dimensional quality. Take your time on this and add as much or as little as you like—just be sure to always add water and smooth out any hard blotchy areas of paint before it sets. A rule of thumb is to darken the deeper areas, while leaving the higher or more prominent areas untouched. Blend between these two differences well. Let the carving dry overnight. Apply one thin coat of satin polyurethane. After the coat has dried, buff the entire piece with 0000 steel wool to dull out any glossy areas.

6"
(15.2cm)

Wood and Tools

Wood choice

I have used several species of wood for the various projects in this book, and I encourage the reader to do the same. Variety is truly the spice of life, and carving wood is no exception. Many people stick to just basswood because it is easy to carve, easy to paint, and easy to acquire. Admittedly, I use basswood more than any other species in my carving projects, but when I get the chance, or when the project calls for it, I like to try other woods. For the projects in this book, I have used five species of wood: basswood, butternut, mahogany, catalpa, and jelutong.

Basswood

Basswood is probably the most common and popular of carving woods in the United States. It is soft enough to carve comfortably, but hard enough to hold detail. It has virtually no grain, which makes it ideal for painting, but if done correctly, it also can be finished naturally. Basswood is also plentiful and easy to purchase.

Basswood

Butternut

Butternut

Butternut is a particular favorite of mine. Although considered a hardwood, it is quite easy to carve. Butternut is particularly soft, and has a very prominent and handsome grain. It has a beautiful warm brown color that varies from ring to ring. Care should be taken, though. Sometimes butternut can be brittle and will easily chip out if you twist your tools unnaturally against the grain. Butternut makes for a beautiful natural finish, and can easily take a polyurethane, lacquer, or oil finish. Unfortunately, butternut's availability is dwindling. It is by no means endangered, but 90 percent of the United States' butternut population has been decimated by disease, and it does not come cheap anymore.

Mahogany

Mahogany is truly a pleasure to carve. It generally has a straight grain and is usually free of voids and pockets. It has a reddish-brown color that darkens over time, and displays a beautiful reddish sheen when polished. It has excellent workability, and is very durable and slow to rot. Mahogany easily takes any number of finishes. Old mahogany can turn quite brittle, and care must be taken when carving; small parts can snap off easily. Being a foreign wood, mahogany can be quite expensive to purchase, depending on the quality and location from which it was derived. The most commonly available variety comes from Honduras.

Catalpa

Catalpa, also known as catawba, is also a personal favorite of mine. Found in many areas of the U.S., it grows large and quite plentiful. It is soft to carve yet quite durable, and is weather resistant. It is not widely known as a carving wood, and is mainly used as a large ornamental shade tree. The grain is very prominent with a color varying from warm brown to grayish-brown, and is often mistaken for butternut. Catalpa takes any number of finishes well. Because there is no commercial use for the lumber, you may have difficulty finding it at a hardwood supplier. Some do carry it, however. Catalpa can be found on the fly, either from someone cutting one down in his or her yard, or after a storm. Catalpa trees grow quite large, with big, heavy limbs. Violent storms often bring them crashing down. Check with your local woodcarver's club; often some of the members have a good source.
It is worth seeking out!

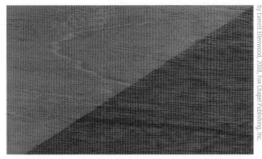

Mahogany

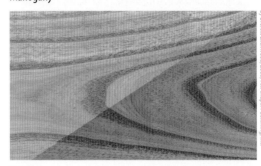

Catalpa

Jelutong

Jelutong

Jelutong is a Southeast Asian tropical wood. It has a low density, and is straight-grained with absolutely no figure at all, making it great for painting. Jelutong is an excellent carving wood; it is soft enough to whittle with a knife, but fine-grained enough to hold detail. It is creamy white to pale yellow in color, and takes any finish; however, it absorbs a great deal of the product before filming on the surface. As scarce as it is, it is surprising to know most woodcarvers have heard of it. The only place I can find it for purchasing is on the Web.

Outside use

Some of you may wish to create the projects in this book to be used as actual waterspouts and outside ornaments, as their ancestors were. Unfortunately, wood does not hold up well when exposed to the elements. Though some original Gothic gargoyles and grotesques were carved from wood, they deteriorated much faster than their stone brethren; very few still survive today. However, if you still want to try to create a functional wooden gargoyle, you will need to finish it with a lot of spar or marine urethane, which is glossy and not very attractive. Additionally, carvings would have to be very large to be of any real use. Purely ornamental carvings could be smaller and placed in a sheltered area. In that case, heavy oil coats on the right type of wood would work, as well as being attractive.

For outside carvings, I suggest cedar, which does not rot, though it does weather to a silver-grey—like the huge totem poles found in the Pacific Northwest. All cedar species (Western red, Northern white, Eastern aromatic, and redwood) are fairly soft and contain a natural oil that resists decay and insects. Cedar is easy to carve, but can be a bit brittle—your tools must be extra sharp. Admittedly, some species are quite hard to locate for purchasing, depending on where you live. Larger pieces of the red varieties will be much easier to find for those who live near the American West Coast and Canada; otherwise, the wood will probably need to be shipped to you. White and aromatic varieties can be found in the eastern U.S., but do not grow nearly as large. All species contain many knots. Since the wood is oily, carving through a knot isn't too difficult. However, the presence of many knots will certainly have a visual impact on the finished piece.

Using patterns

You will want to photocopy the patterns from this book to use as a template. Most of the patterns require enlargement, so I have marked the photocopy size on them. Cut out the pattern and trace it onto the block of wood you have prepared, making sure the front and side line up. Also, be sure to lay out the pattern with the grain as indicated. The grain direction is marked on the pattern pages. The dimensions for the wood blank are noted for each project. Several of the projects are such that only one view is needed for sawing. In those cases, the other views are for reference only.

Some of the project patterns in this book are complex to band saw. If you are new to this, don't be intimidated or discouraged. Just take your time and plan your cut before plunging in. Be sure to cut out small bites at a time, and leave extra wood around small protrusions. Practicing on scrap wood first can help, if you feel the need. Most people own nothing bigger than a 14" (35.6cm) band saw, so I have limited either the width or the height of the blank to 6" (15.2cm)—close to the clearance limit from table to blade guard. This comes in handy if you need to cut down the thickness of your wood stock when preparing the blank. Do not use a blade any wider than ¼" (6mm) when sawing out the patterns. If you own or have access to a larger saw, feel free to enlarge the pattern and carve a bigger project! Of course, if you do not feel comfortable sawing out some of these patterns, have a more experienced person do it for you. Always remember to wear goggles and practice safety at all times.

You will need a vise or clamping system of some kind to execute these carvings. I designed this bench with a ball-type rotating carver's vise.

Using a vise

Due to the moderately complex pattern shapes of the projects in this book, I have used a clamping system to hold them in place while carving. I strongly suggest the same for you. Most of the projects are either too unwieldy or have too many delicate parts to be hand-held. Another reason to clamp is to free both of your hands. Hogging out excess wood will be best accomplished with gouges rather than knives, for the most part. Once the project is well underway, some details could then be applied while the carving is hand-held.

Any carver's homemade or store-bought vise or clamping system will do. You can use a simple carpenter's vise, which is built-in on most workbenches, combined with bench dogs to wedge the project in place. If you will be using a common machine vise, be sure to line the inside of the jaws with some thin pieces of basswood; anything harder, and the carving will be marred. For the step-by-step projects, I used a carving bench of my own design. This bench, when combined with a ball-type rotating carver's vise, allows me to sit and bend over my work. The carving can be positioned in any manner possible, frees my hands to use gouge and mallet, and is comfortable enough to sit for hours without back strain.

A moderate variety of tools is needed to complete these projects. You should have shallow gouges, half-round gouges, fishtails, V-tools, skew chisels, veiners, and knives.

Carving tools

As far as most of the projects in this book are concerned, the tool requirement is moderate to extensive. I use shallow gouges, half-round gouges, fishtails, V-tools, skew chisels, veiners of various sizes, and of course, several knives. My personal course of action for these projects is as follows: with the blade securely held in a vise, rough out with a larger shallow gouge and possibly a mallet. Next, switch to medium-sized gouges and a variety of knives to work the piece into shape. Finally, apply details with small palm gouges and more knife-work.

A sharp tool is essential. You'd think this goes without saying, but there are many beginners who struggle on a piece of wood only to give up in frustration. They blame themselves, thinking they don't have what it takes, when all along a dull tool is the culprit. To carve with the sharpest of tools is a joy that must be experienced to be appreciated.

Learning to successfully sharpen is an art unto itself. It's practically half the battle when learning to carve. It took several years for me to become comfortable with my own sharpening skills, and I tried many different stones and accessories. I finally bought a motorized wet grinder. I get an edge fast, but I have to be careful not to end up with a little nub for a tool. Fortunately, you don't need one of these to do a good job. I prefer to sharpen my knives by hand, leaving the grinder for the gouges. The job is easy with a pair of medium and fine ceramic stones. It would take a whole chapter or two to go over sharpening specifics, so I suggest purchasing a good sharpening book from your local or mail order carving supply store if you are not already accustomed to sharpening your own tools successfully.

Other tools and techniques

For some of the projects, life can be made easier with the help of some other tools such as a hand drill, a drill press (if available), a pull saw, clamps (for gluing), and a rotary grinder with bits. Not all of these are required, but remember there is a tool for every purpose, and the more you have, the more efficient you can become.

Wood softener

As most carvers know, sometimes a given wood species is not as soft as you might prefer. Sometimes the grade isn't so great, but it's all you've got. Sometimes you have a lot of detail to carve right into the end grain, and no matter how sharp your tool is, it still seems to tear the fibers instead of slicing through them. Prepare a 50/50 mixture of water and isopropyl alcohol, put it in a spray or mister bottle, and spray it lightly on the area being worked. Let it soak in a few moments, and then spray it again. Start carving! The tool should glide through the stubborn wood much easier. I'm not sure how or why it works, but it does. I use it almost every time I need to carve end grain.

Cyanoacrylate

Cyanoacrylate, otherwise known as crazy glue or instant glue, is another handy tool to have around. It's perfect for that desperate moment when you accidentally break off a fragile piece, or chip out a chunk that should have stayed in place. Within moments of application, you're back in business. Try to stay away from the popular hardware store brands, which can be inferior in quality. Look instead for specialty brands found in woodworking stores, catalog, or hobby shops. Instant glue is also excellent for reinforcing an otherwise fragile area. Simply apply the glue to the desired area and let it soak in. Within minutes, it will be twice as strong as before.

A word of caution: cyanoacrylates are volatile substances. The fumes will make your eyes and sinuses burn almost instantly, especially when bending over your work. Also, it will adhere anything to anything else, including your hand to the table. Wear gloves, a mask, perhaps goggles, and use in a well-ventilated area.

Finishing techniques

Several of the finishes for projects in this book are simple clear coats. I have used a few unconventional methods as well. Because these projects are all reproductions of subjects that would originally been carved of stone, this gives us a great creative freedom.

Polyurethane

Polyurethane is an oil-based varnish. It is easy to apply, durable, and adds a slight amber tone. Purchase satin, not gloss. Gloss reflects a lot of light, gives a plastic look, and distracts from the details of the piece. I choose to thin out the satin poly with mineral spirits to make it even less apparent. You can thin it yourself or buy a wipe-on poly.

When applying, it is best to sand between coats. I suggest using 000 (fine) steel wool or equivalent Scotch-Brite pad instead of sandpaper. It is easier to get into uneven surfaces. Thoroughly clean out the debris before adding the next coat. If you don't, it will forever be locked into the crevices. Buff out the final coat with 0000 (very fine) steel wool. Buffing will dull any glossy areas.

Boiled linseed oil

I use boiled linseed oil as a pre-finish to bring out the grain in the wood. Boiled linseed oil should never be applied full-strength—always make a 50/50 mix with mineral spirits. Apply liberally with a brush, let it soak in for a few minutes, and wipe off the excess. Depending on the wood, it can get soaked up quickly. Applying linseed oil to any raw wood will instantly darken the natural color. Linseed oil can also be tinted by adding artist oil color paint.

Tung oil

Tung oil is a natural oil that can be used as a stand-alone finish. It leaves a soft, hand-rubbed look and makes an excellent alternative to poly. It is not as durable as poly, but if care is taken, it will hold up. Tung oil is typically applied by cloth, but I would suggest using a brush to get into deep areas. You can purchase 100% tung oil or tung oil finish, which contains polymer driers. Do not use more than four applications; more than that, and either will leave a milky, cloudy look. Steel wool can be used between coats.

Lacquer

Lacquer is a favorite of mine, and makes an excellent clear coat. It dries very quickly to a crystal clear. If you keep the coats thin, little sanding is required. More good news is lacquer is easy to repair and sand. Lacquer will actually re-melt the previously applied and dried coat to form one cohesive surface. The downside is the volatile fumes it produces. Proper ventilation should be used in combination with a mask at all times. Lacquer has been known to cause respiratory problems, so if this is a problem for you, stay away.

Acrylic paint

Acrylic paints of the cheap craft variety are great for adding color to any project, and although they are water based, I always use them in combination with oil-based finishes. I like to thin the paint with water as I apply it, so the wood surface still shows through.

Installing keyhole hangers

Some of the projects in this book will need to be hung on a wall or other vertical surface in order to be displayed properly. The most efficient way to do this is to install small metal keyhole hangers, which are common, inexpensive, and found in any hardware store. When installed properly, they will sit flush against the back surface of the carving, and will hang by a screw or nail head driven into the adjoining vertical surface.

1 After finding the center of your carving in the back, trace the outside image of the hanger, as shown. Be sure to center the hanger carefully when tracing.

2 Using a knife and shallow gouge, I have carved a ⅛" (3mm) deep recess. Be sure the hanger fits tightly and flush with the surface. Then, draw in the screw holes and a void area that will encompass the slot area, as shown.

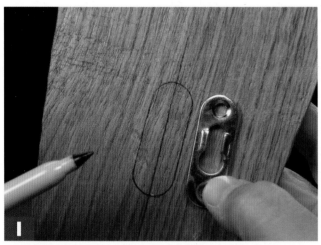

3 Using the knife and shallow gouge, I have recessed the center area another ⅛" (3mm).

4 Attach the hanger by installing the supplied screws, as shown.

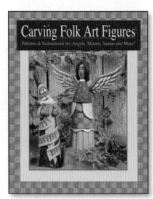
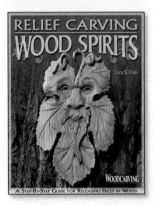
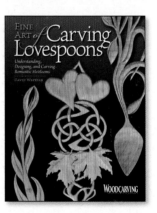